MW01328288

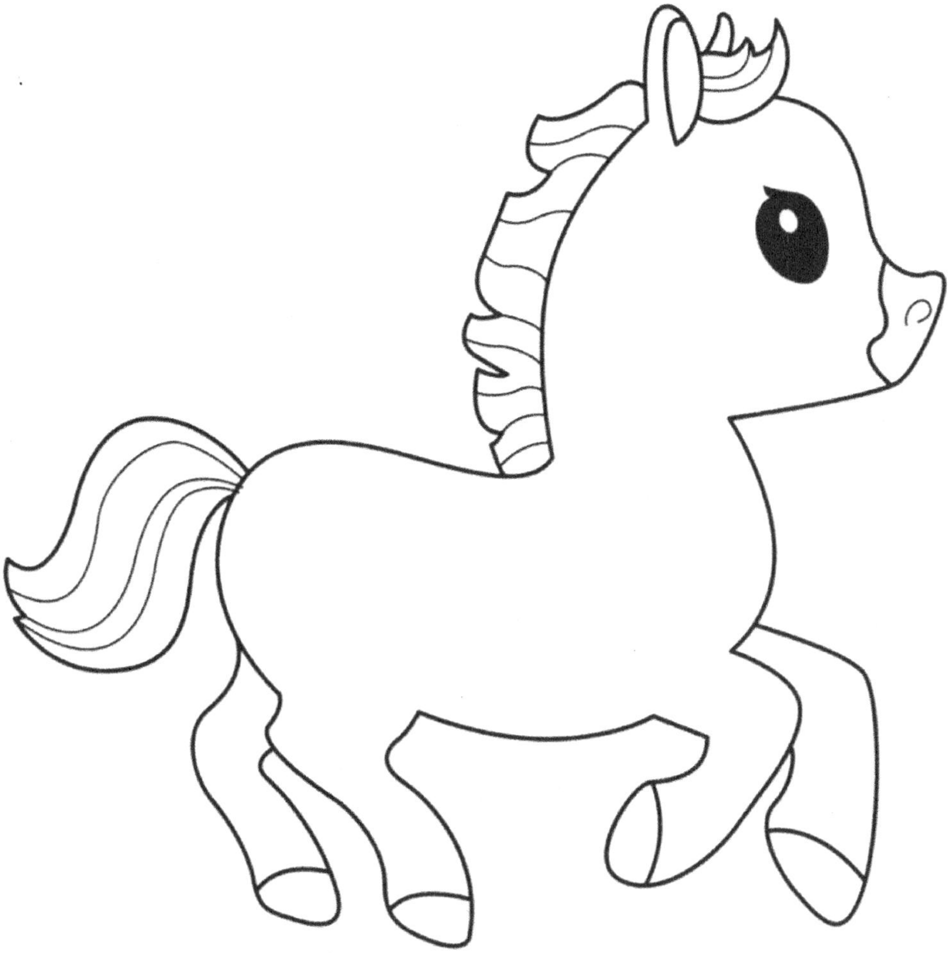

This Book Belongs To

____

An Awesome Artist & Horse Lover

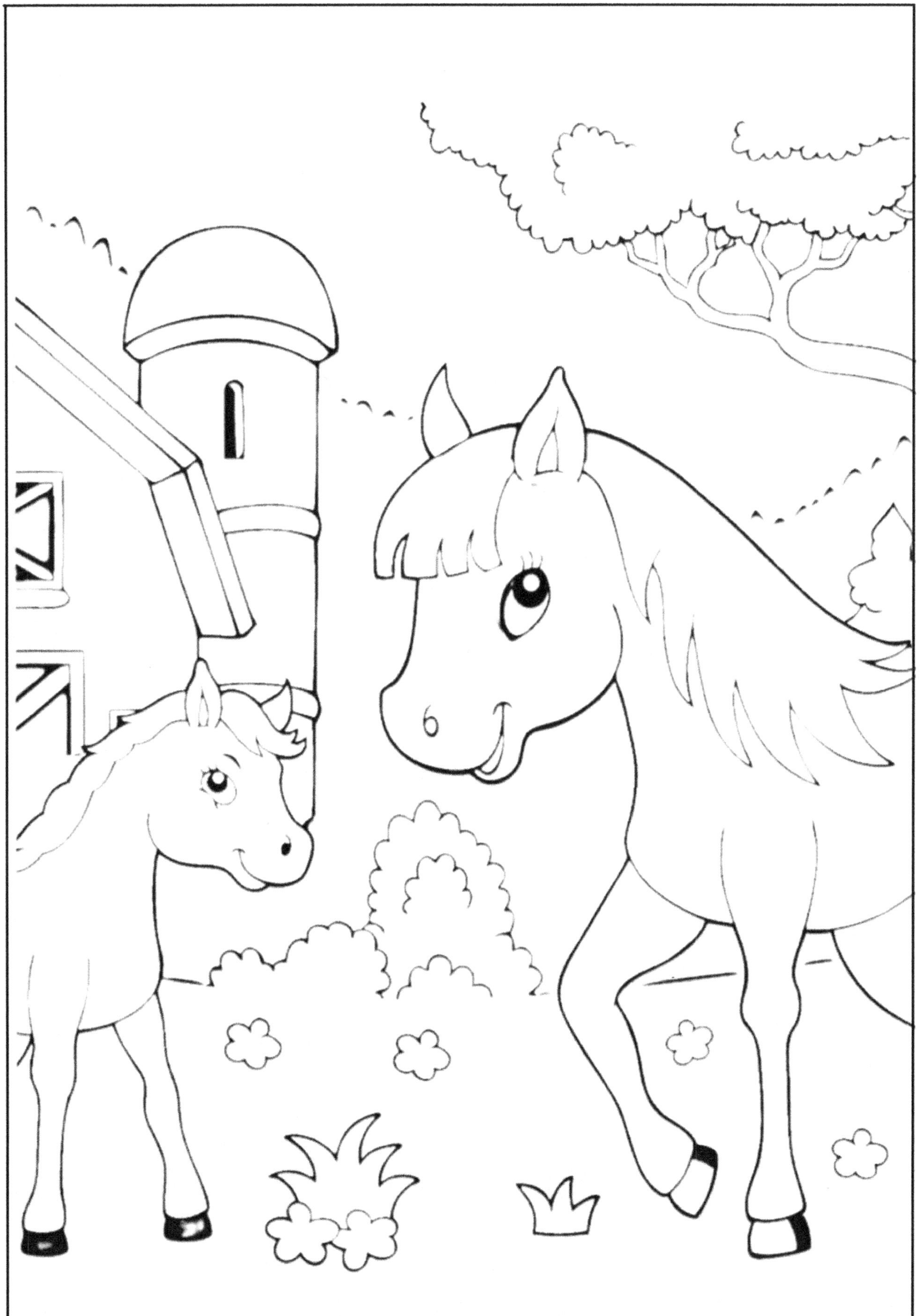

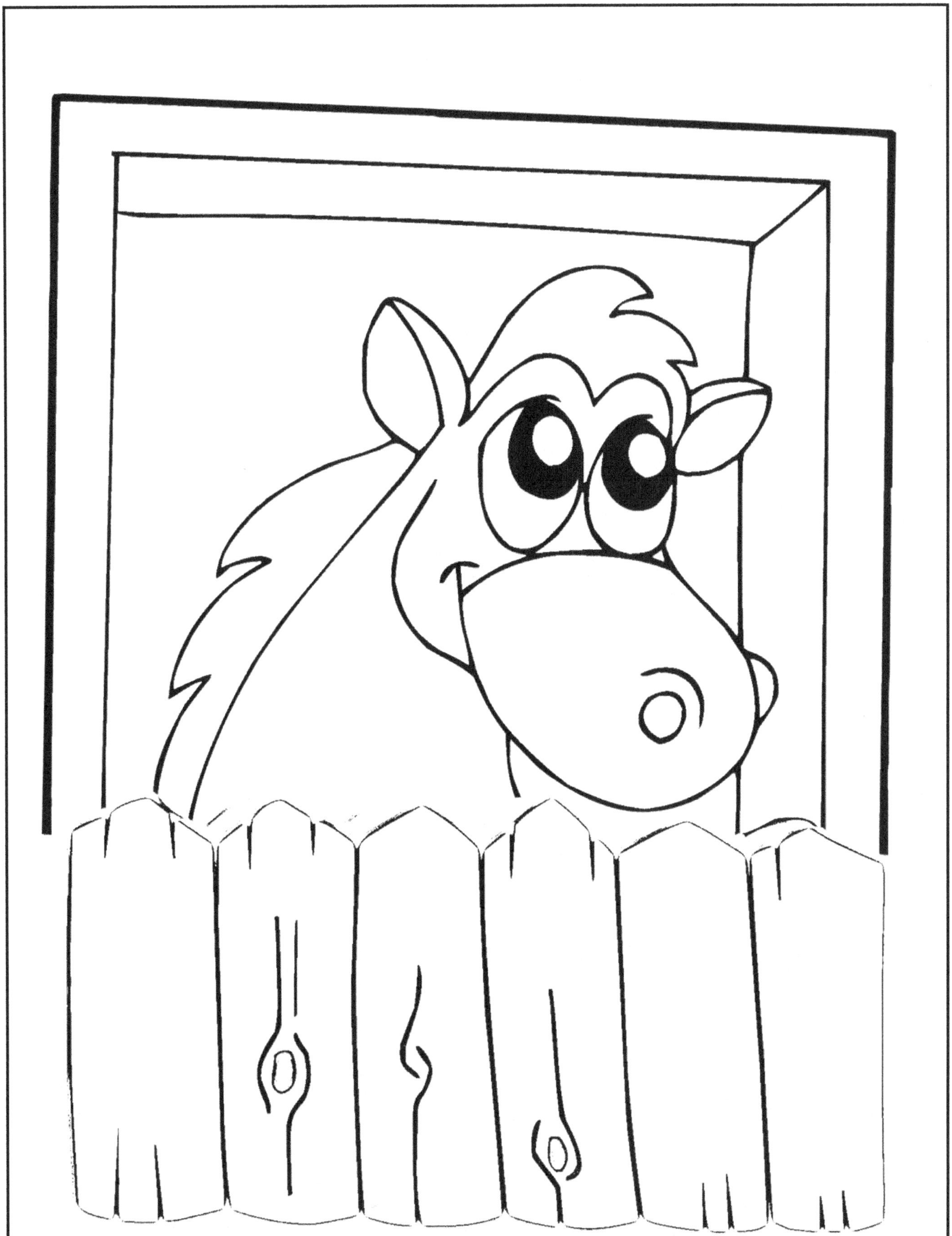

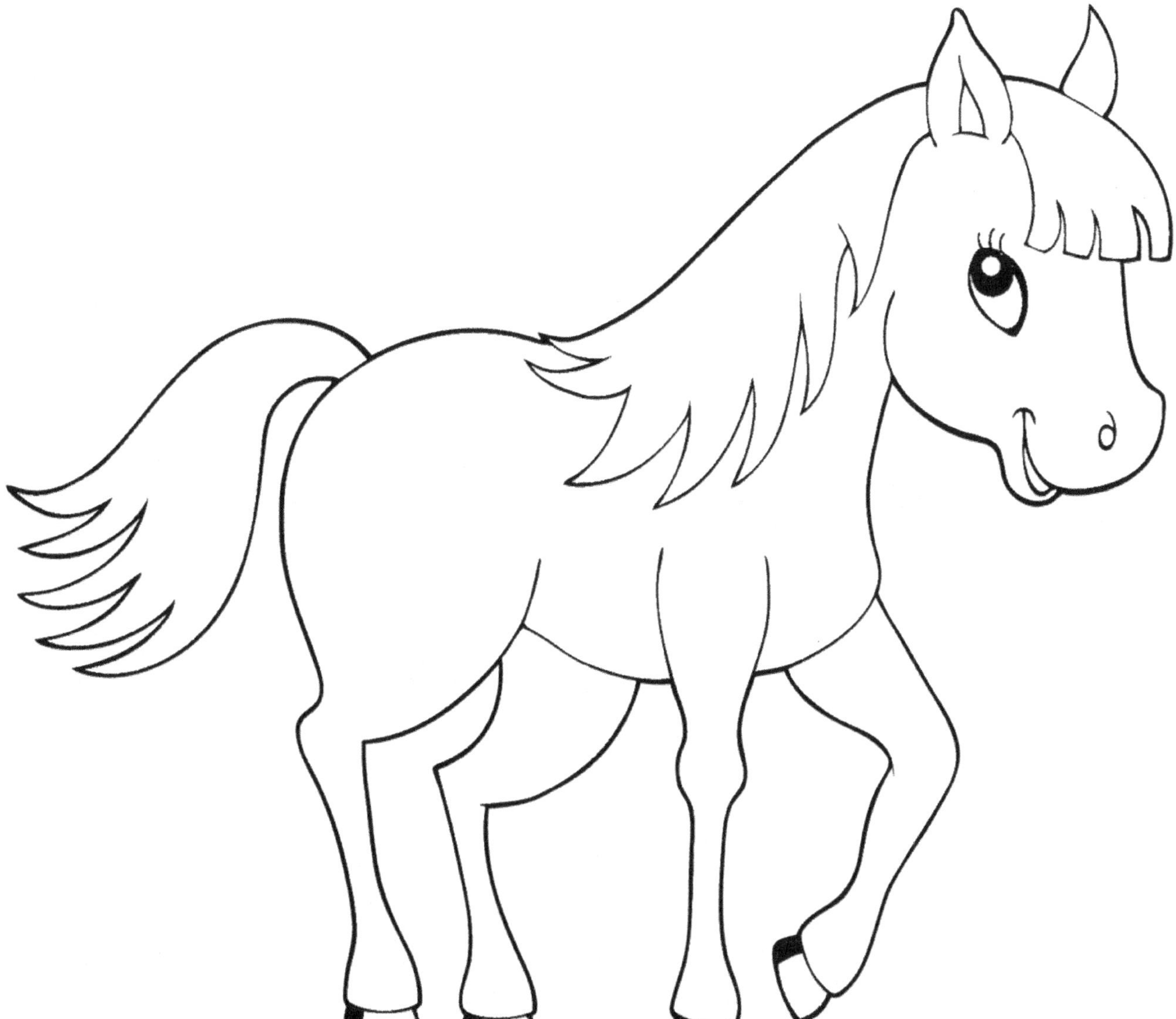

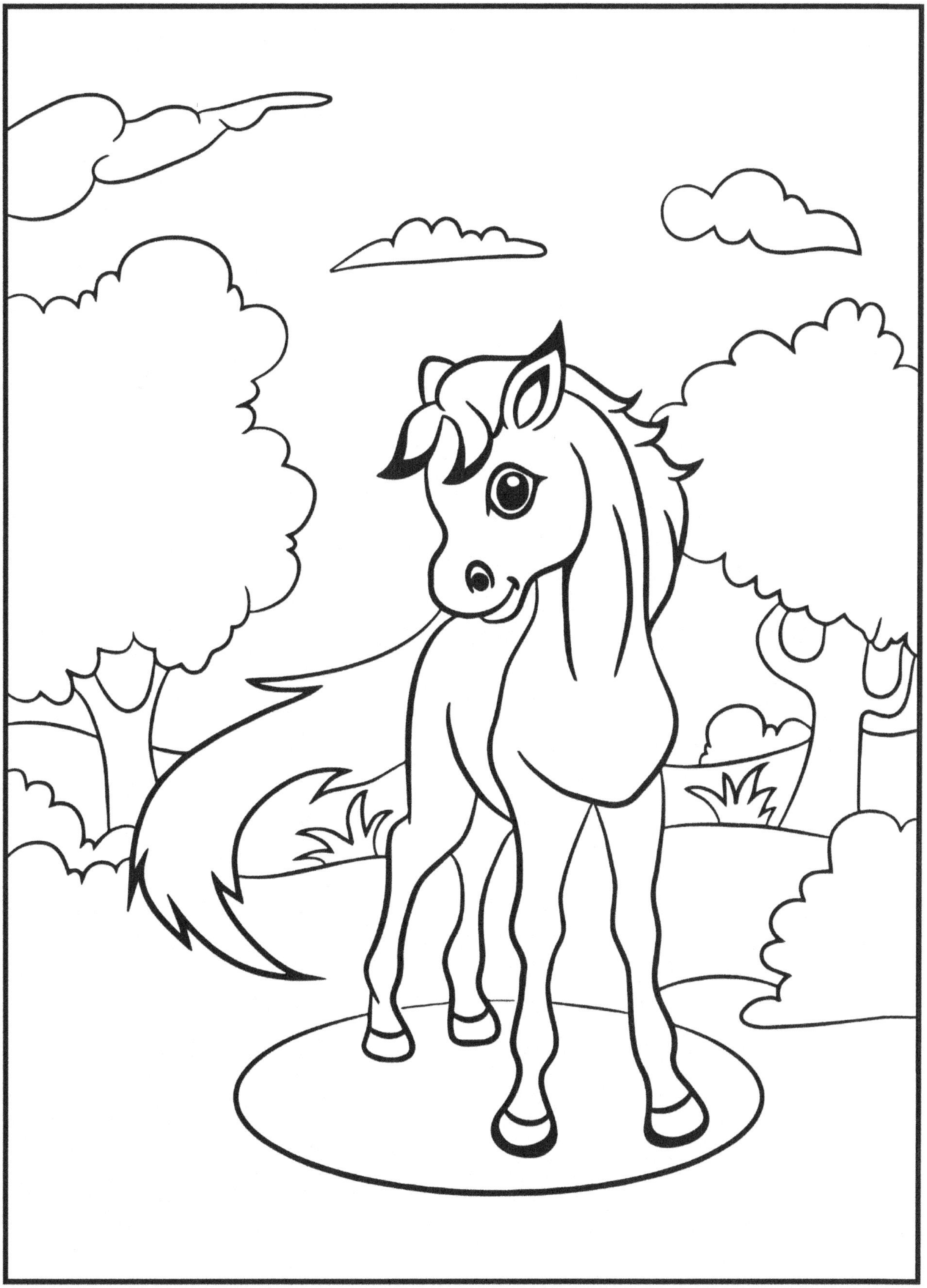

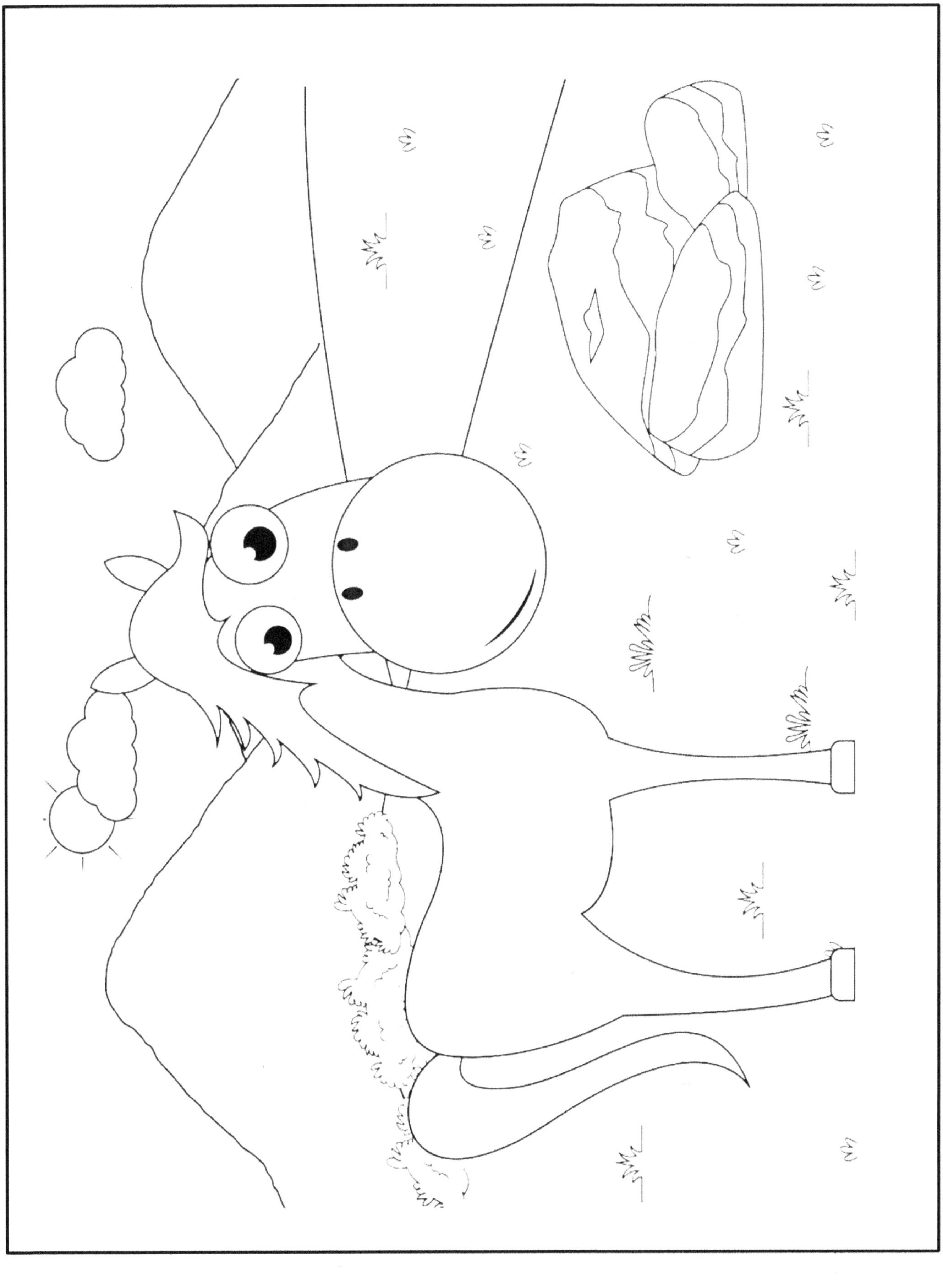

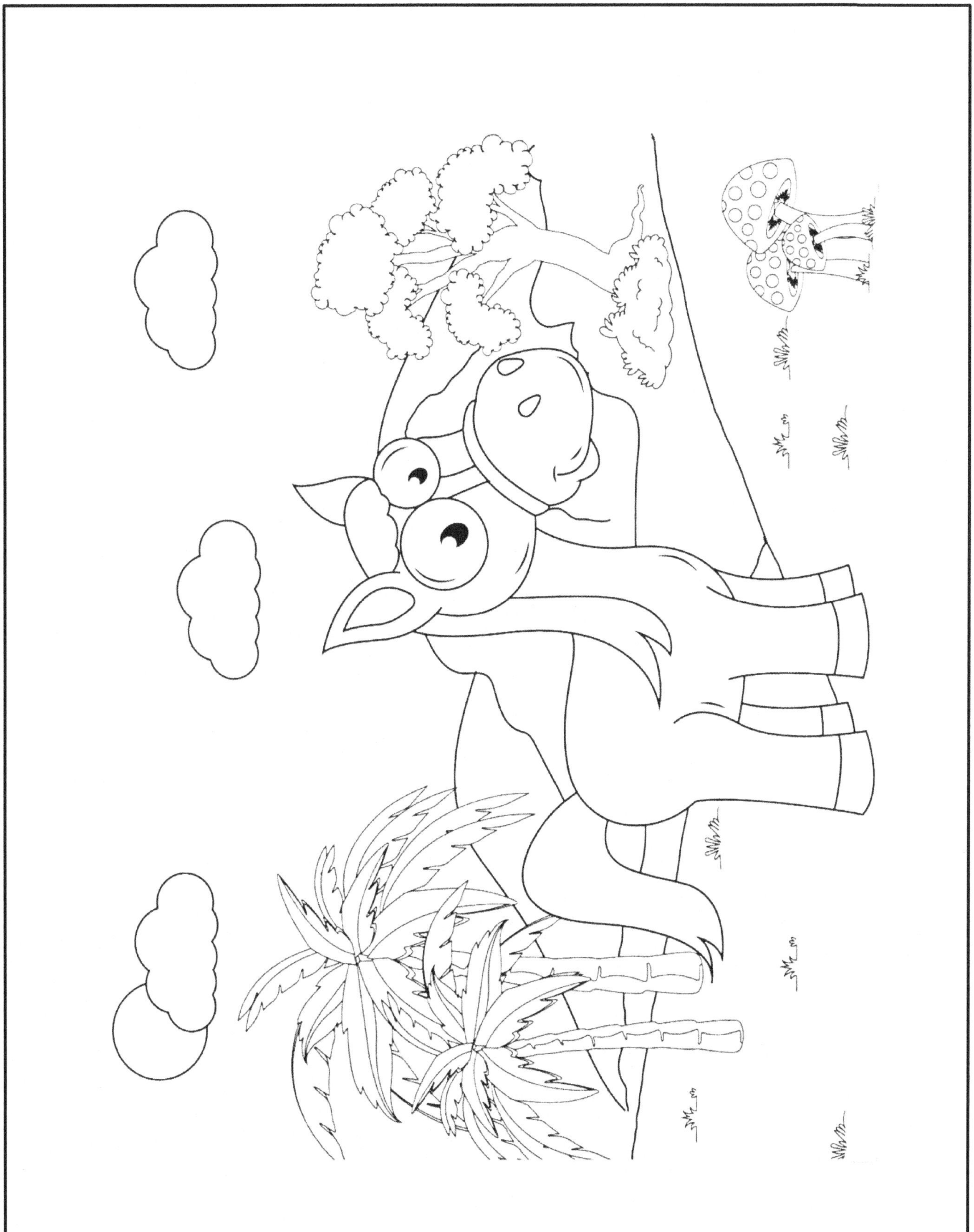

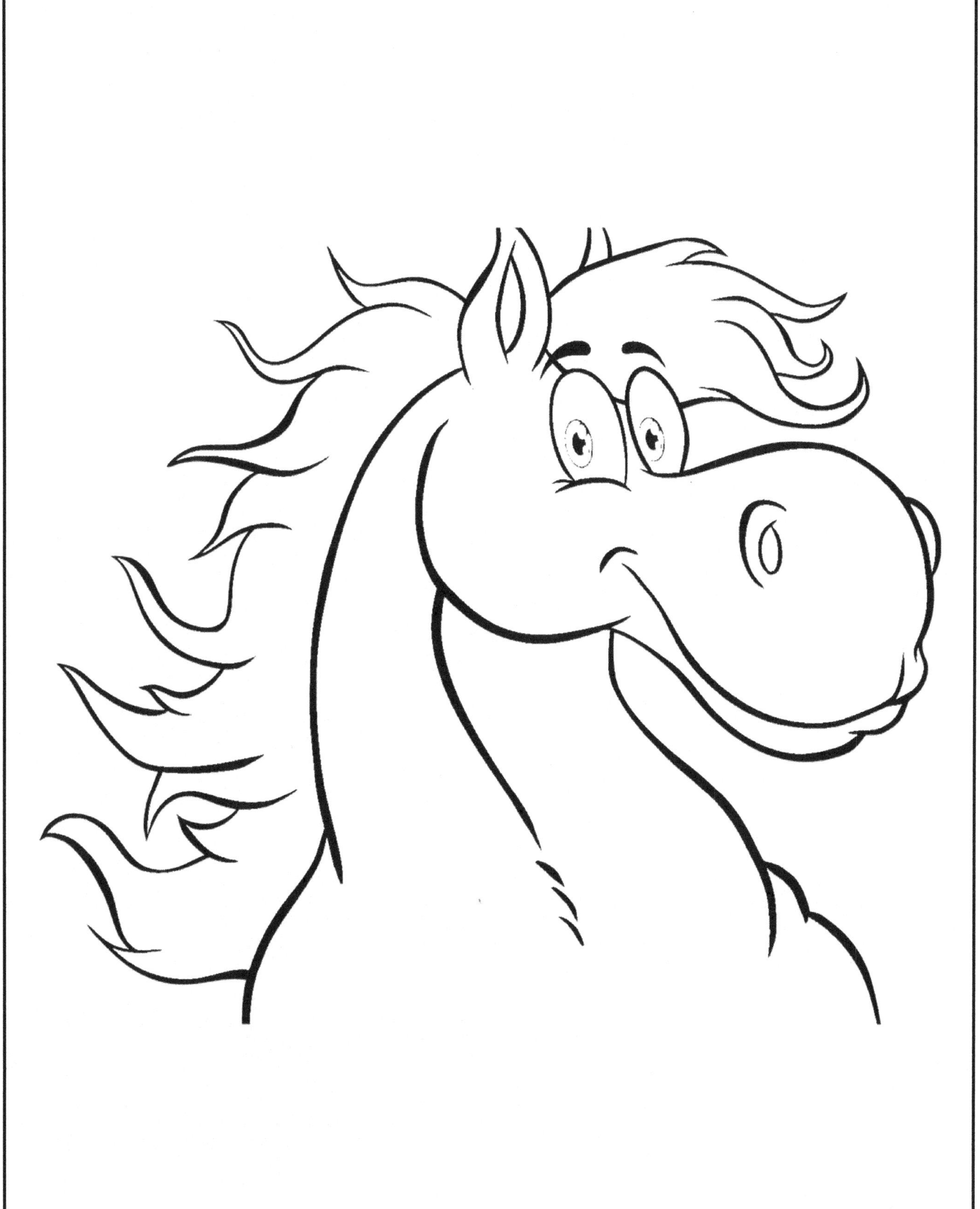

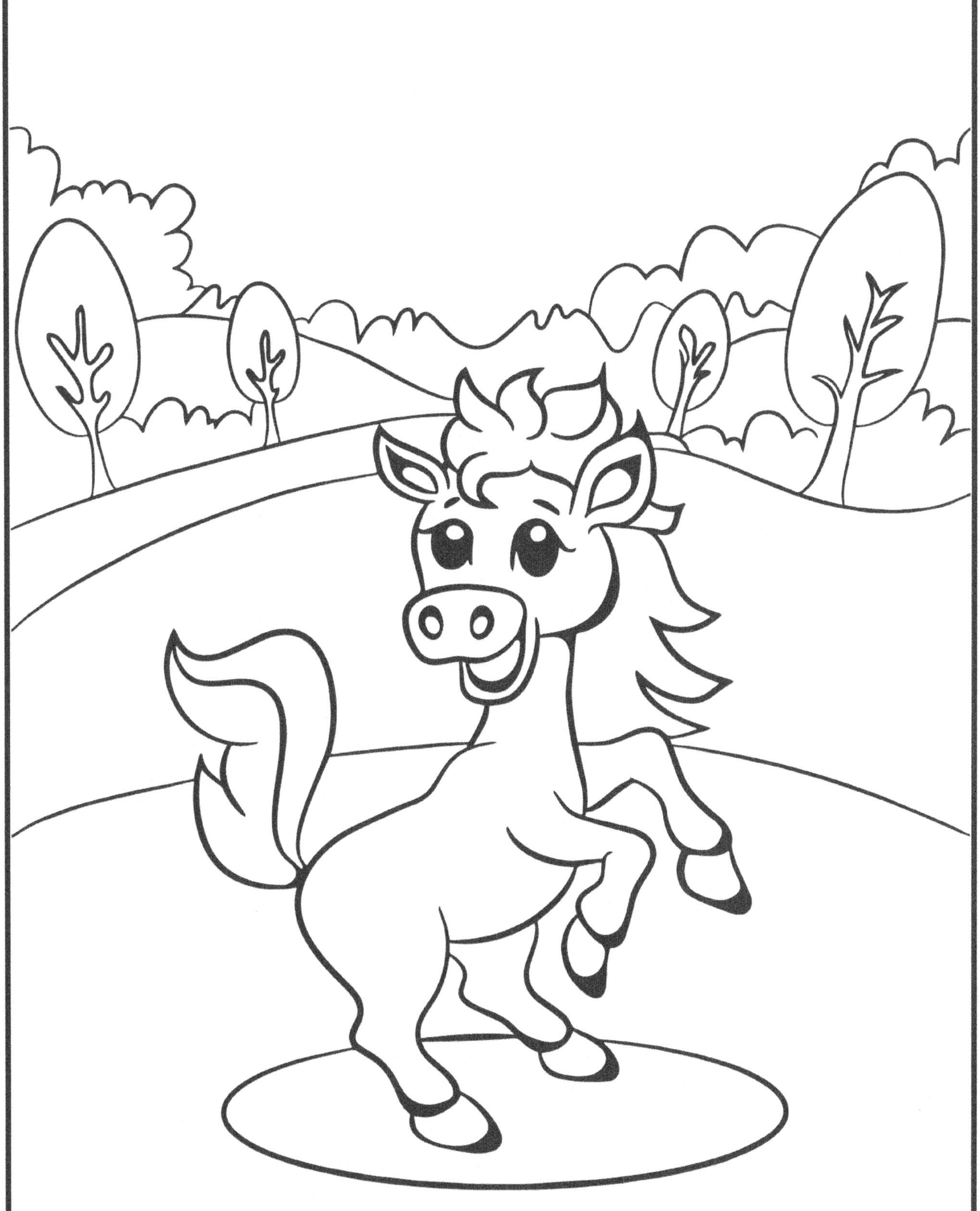

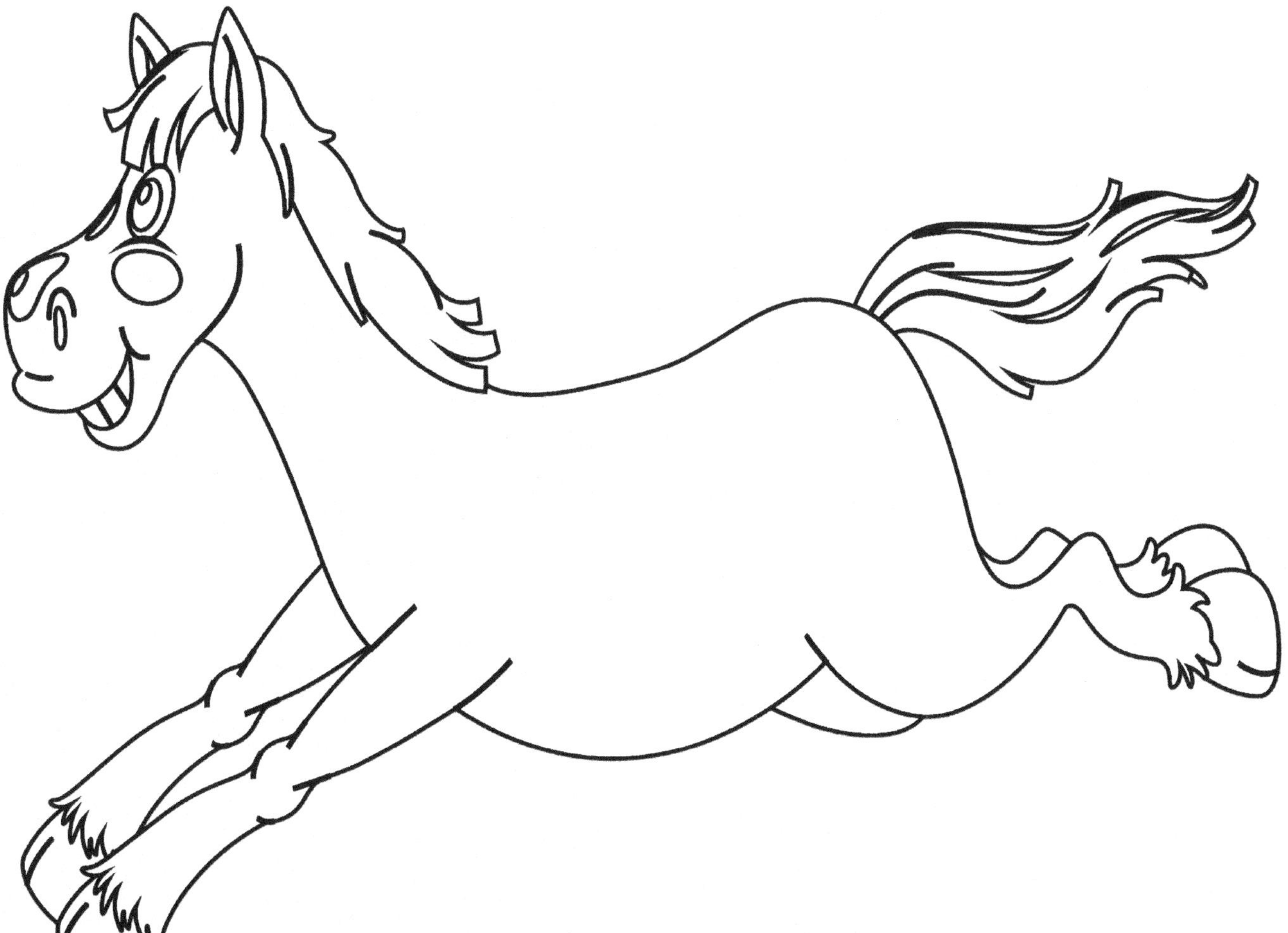

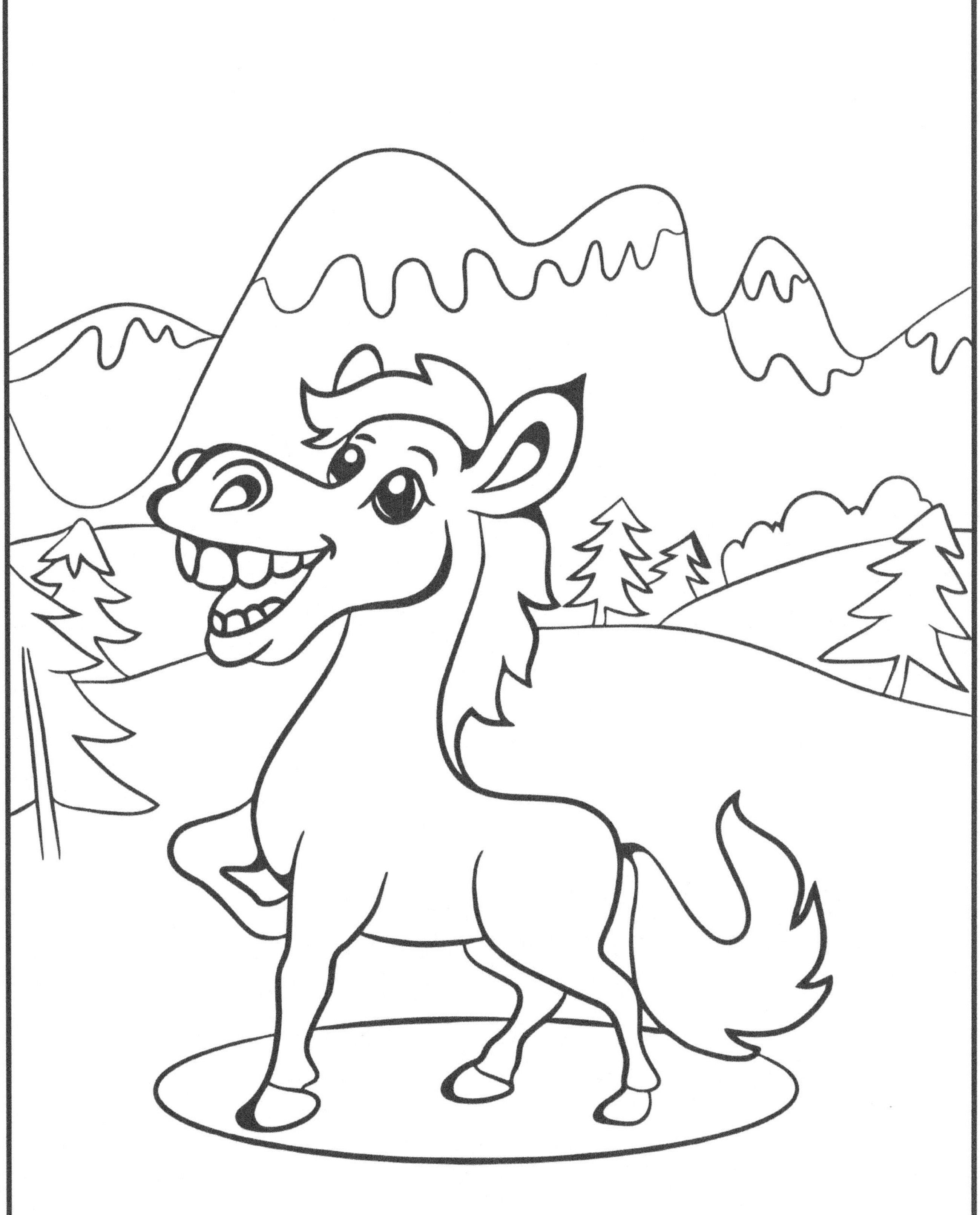

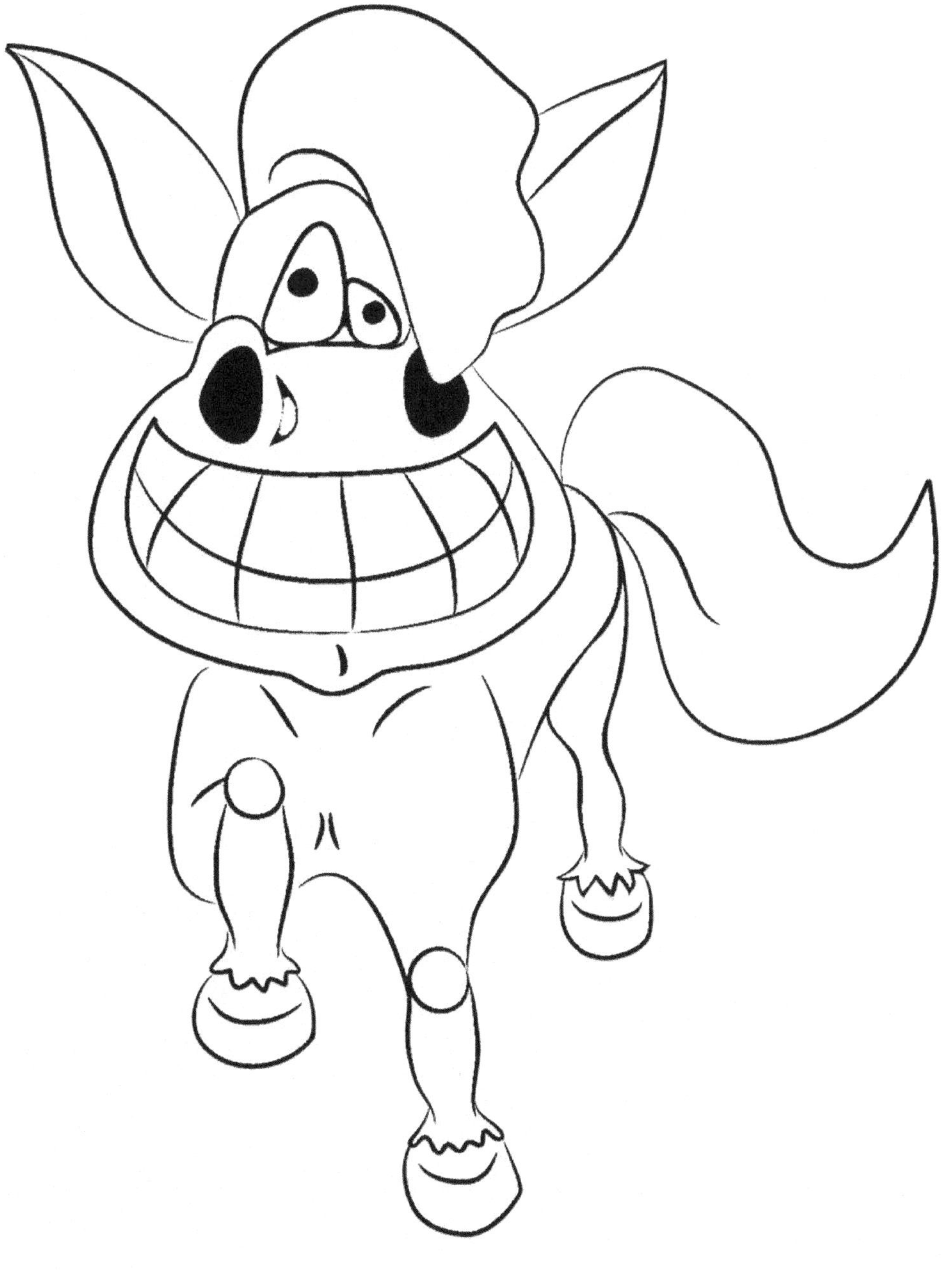

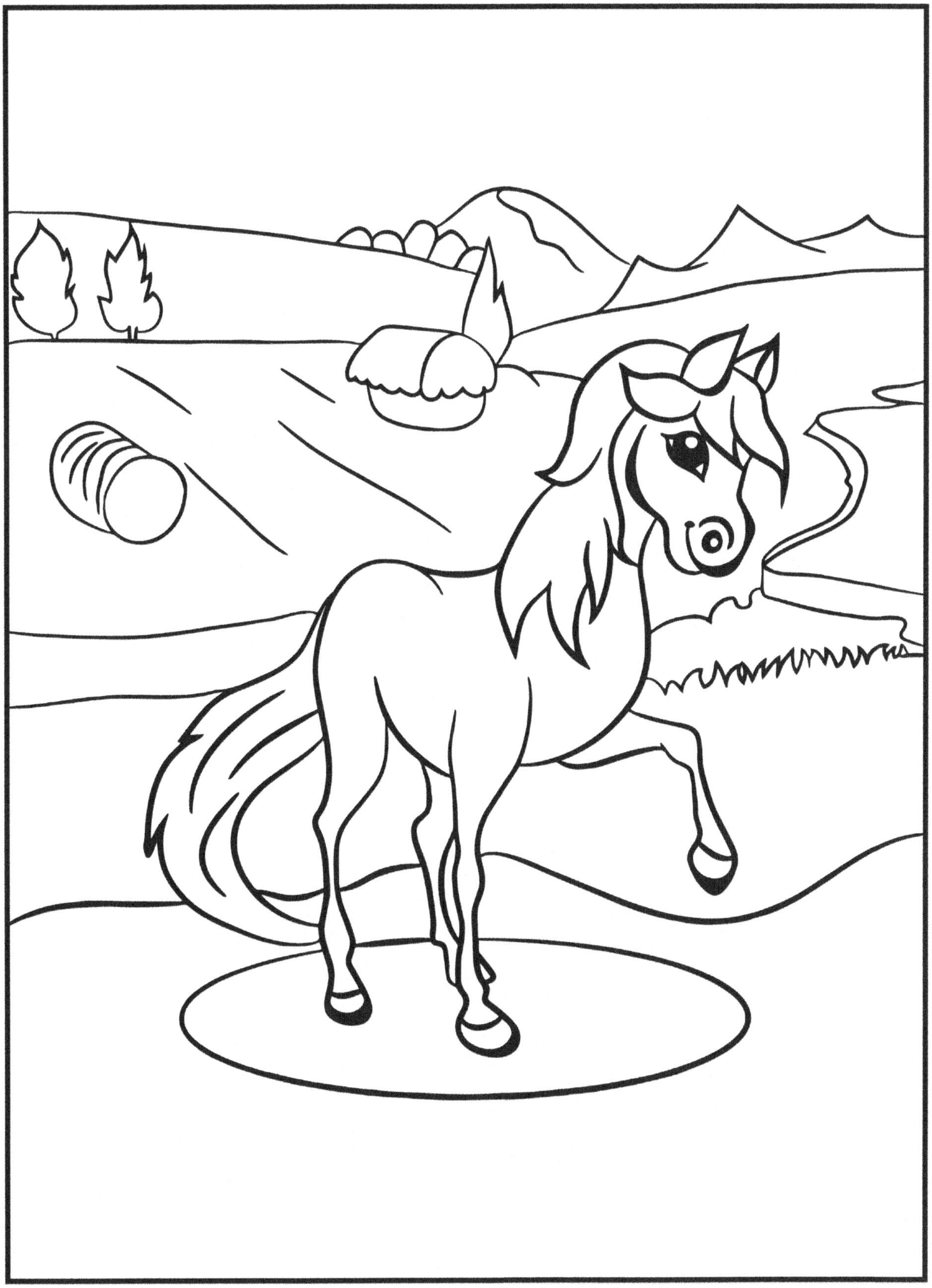

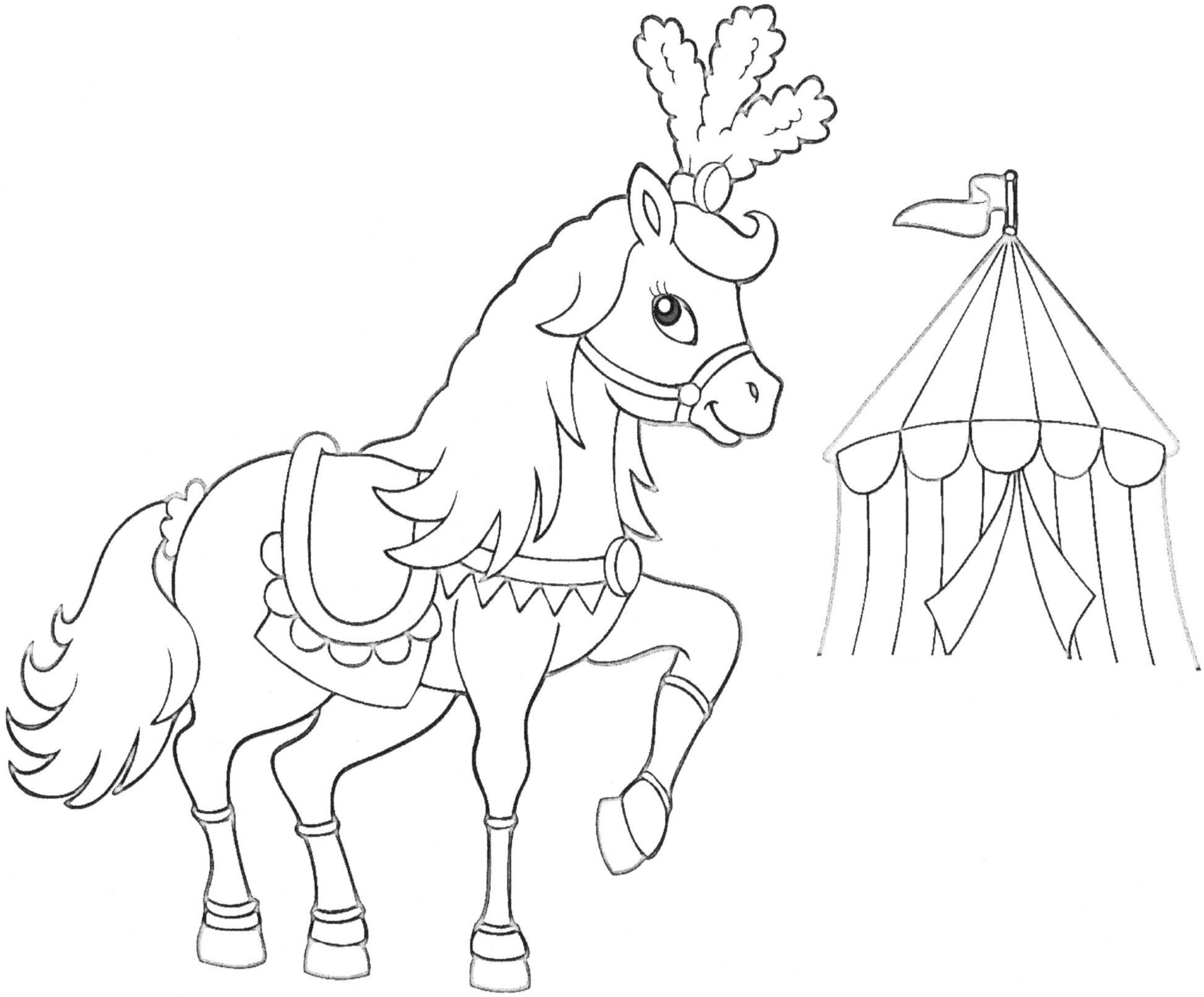

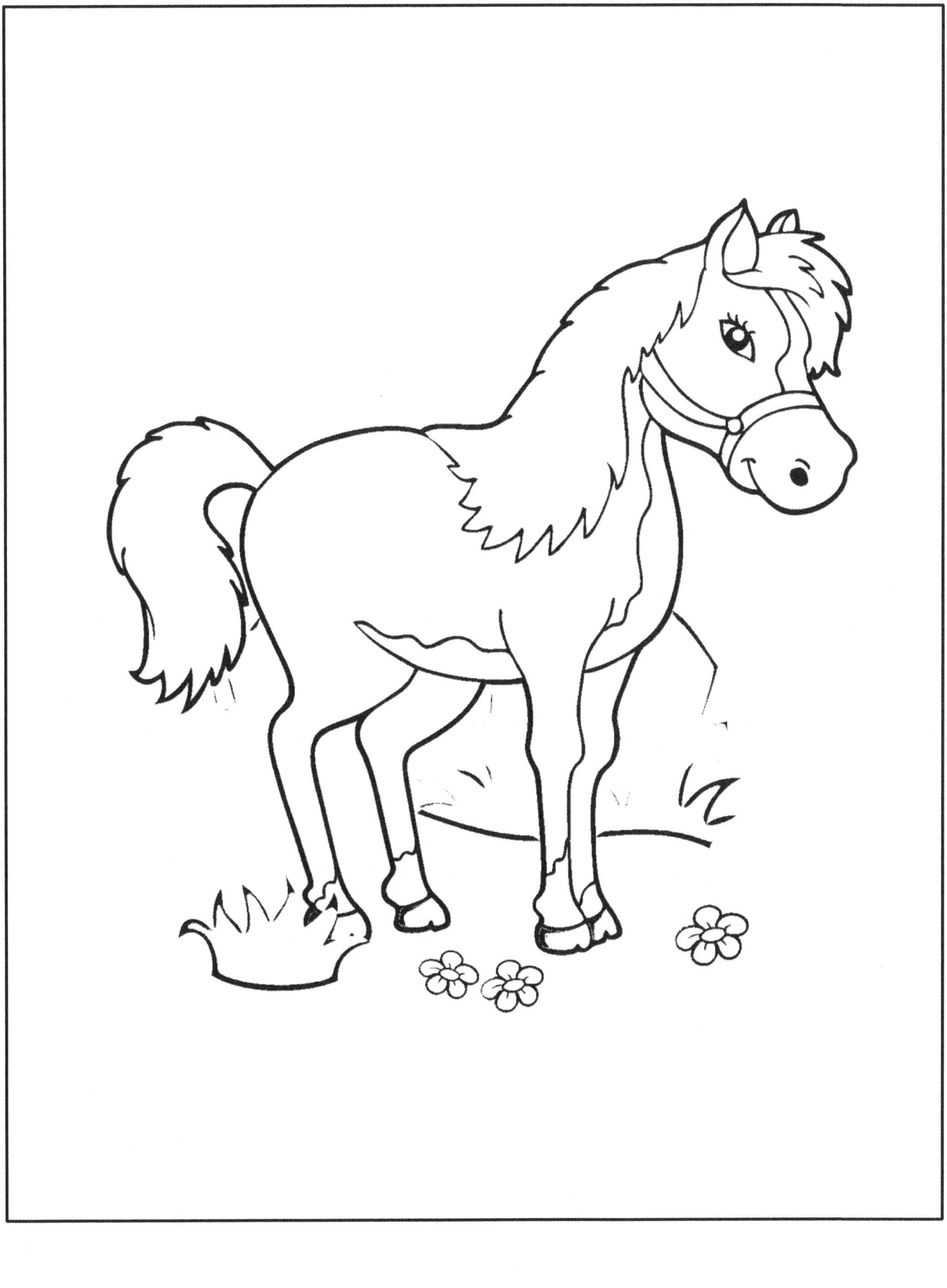

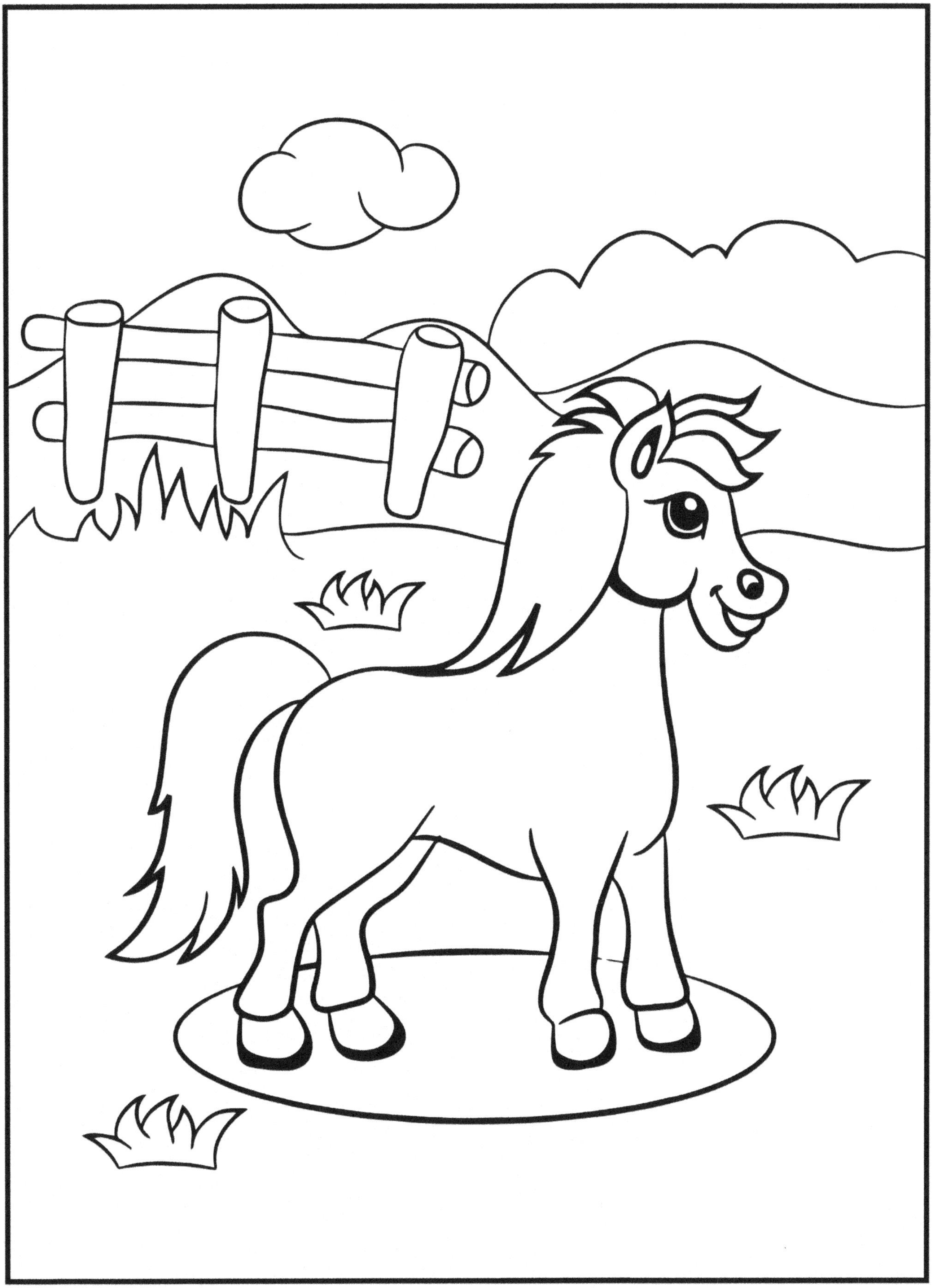

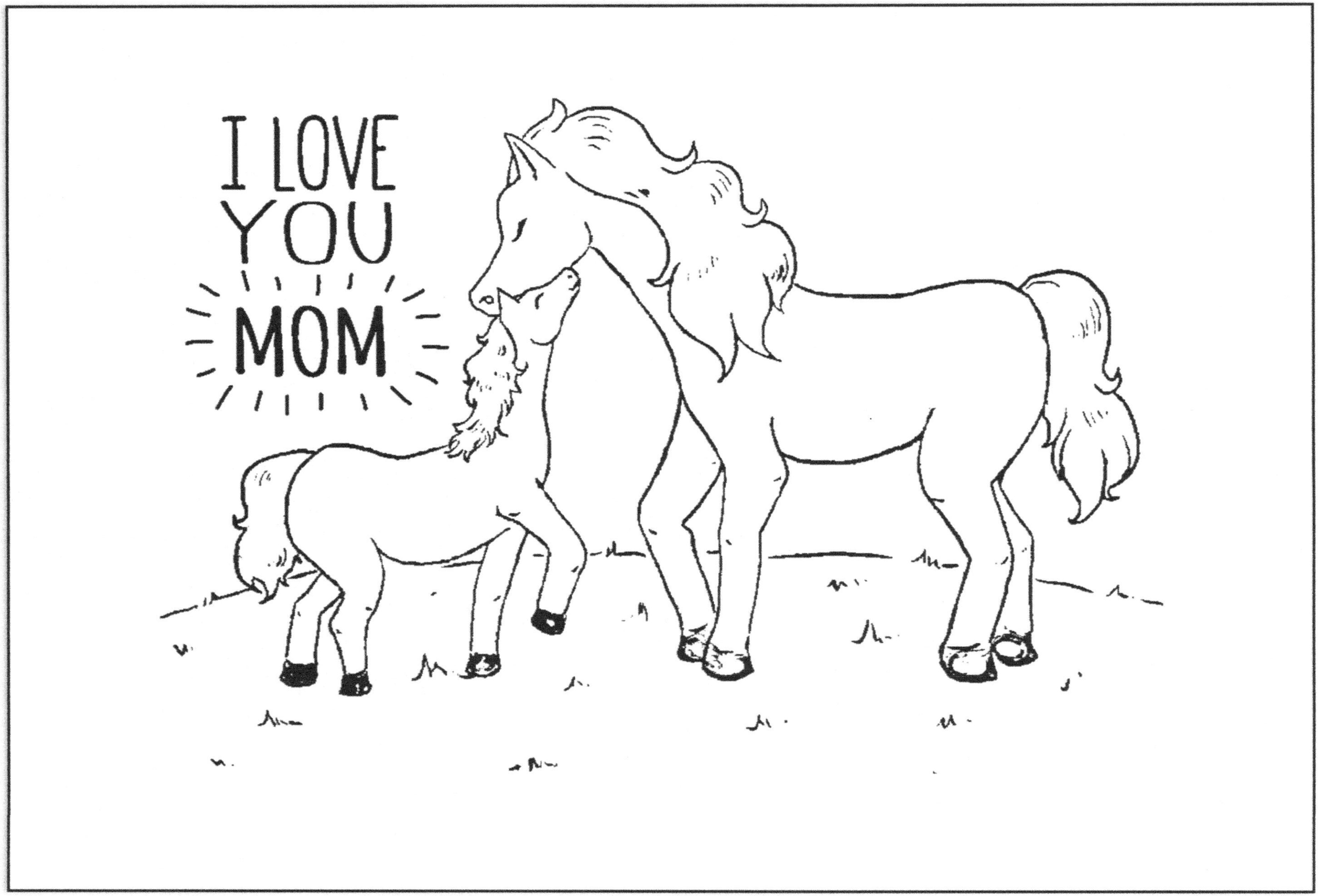
I LOVE YOU MOM

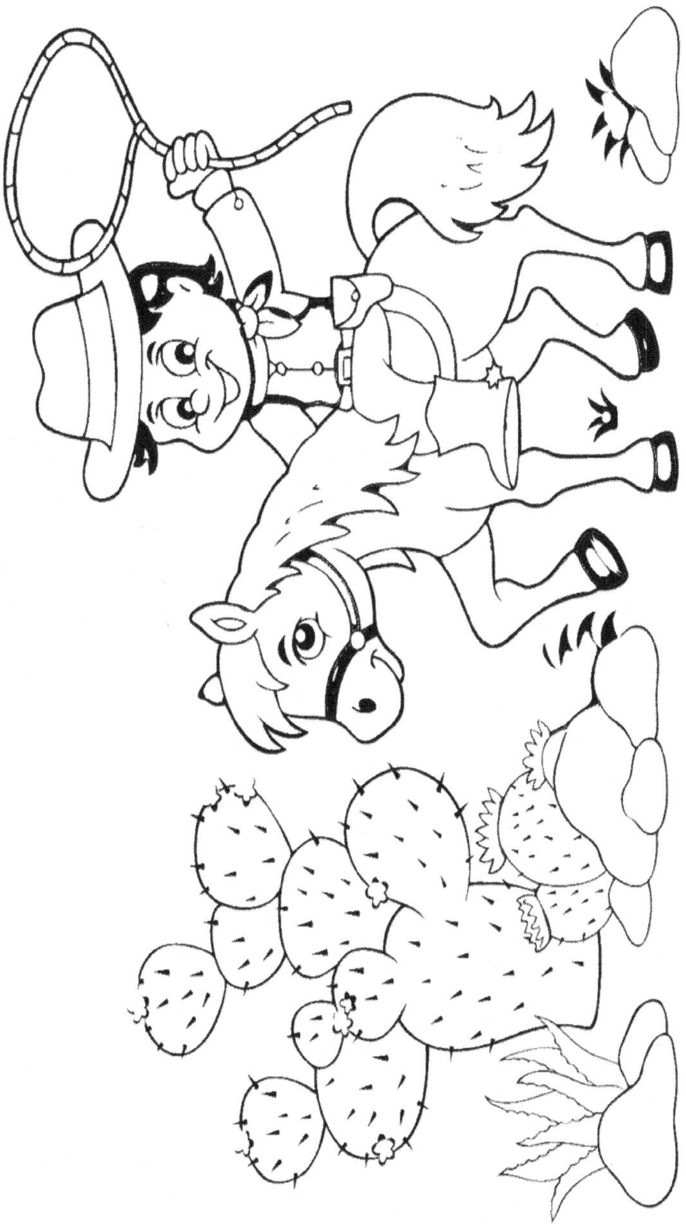

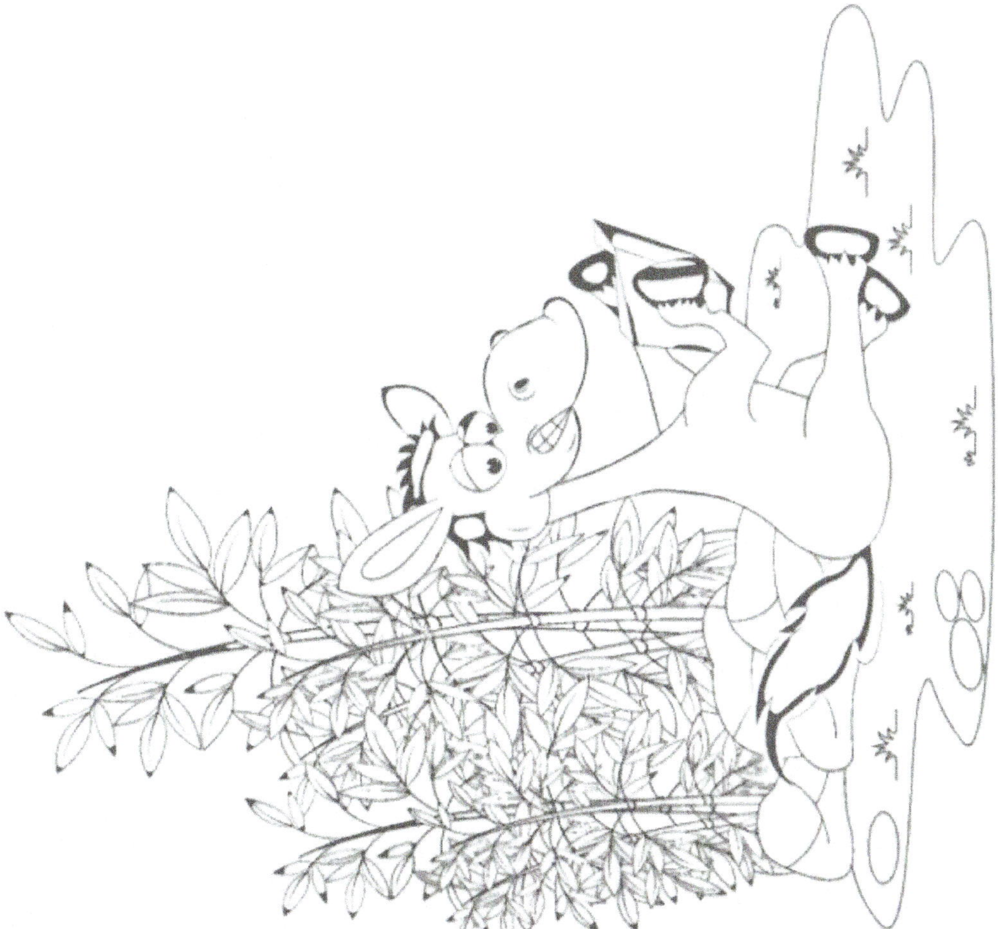

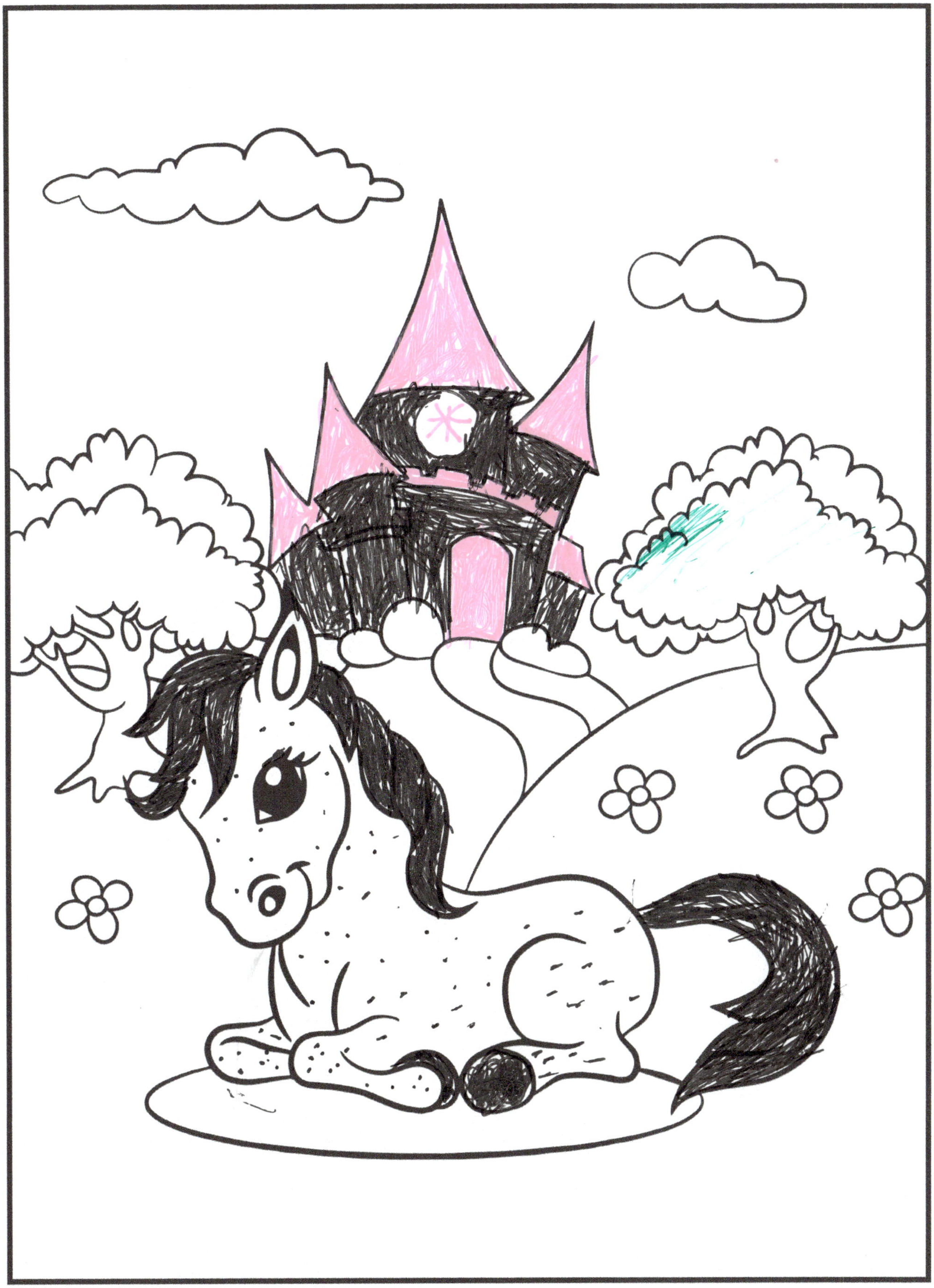

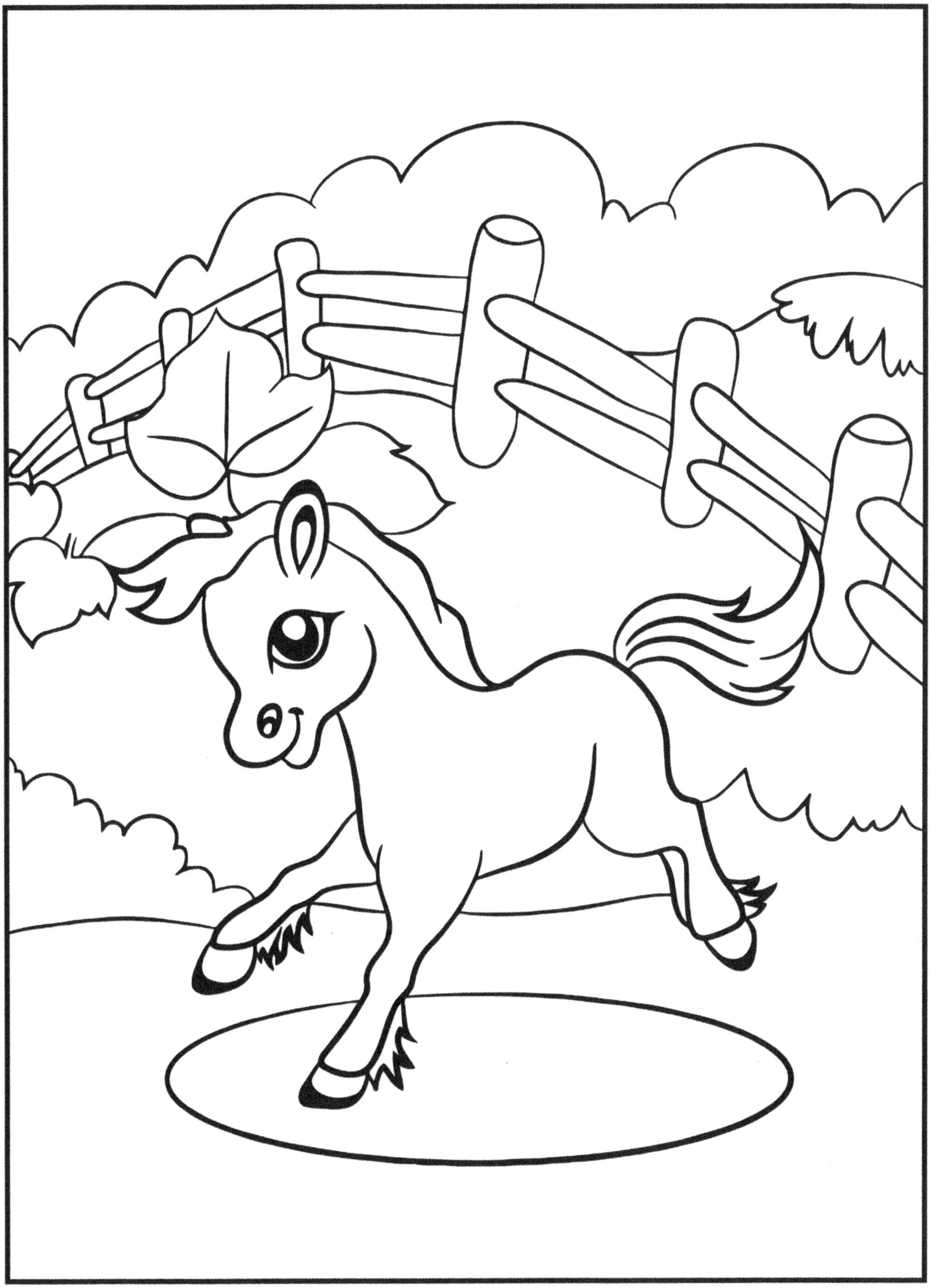

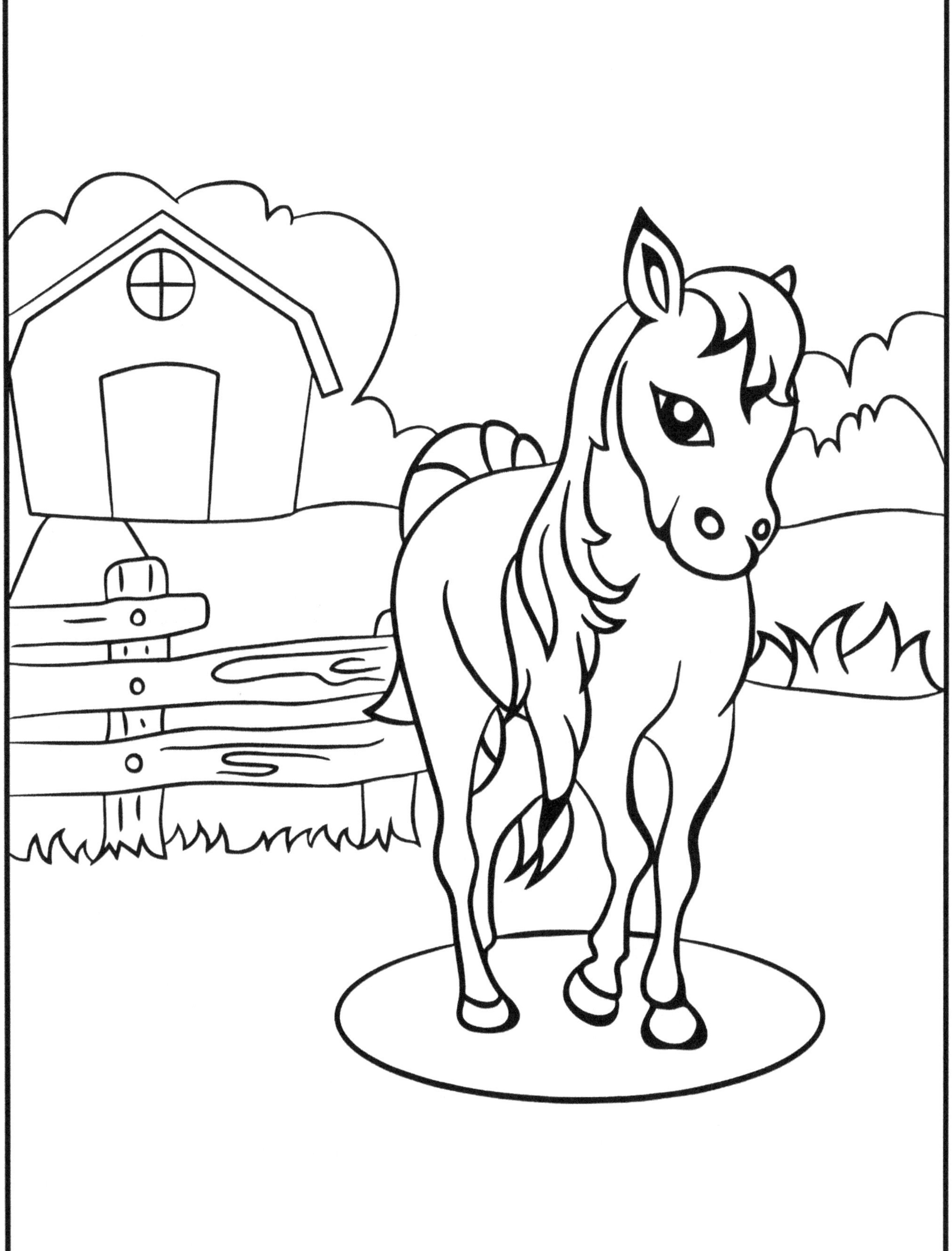

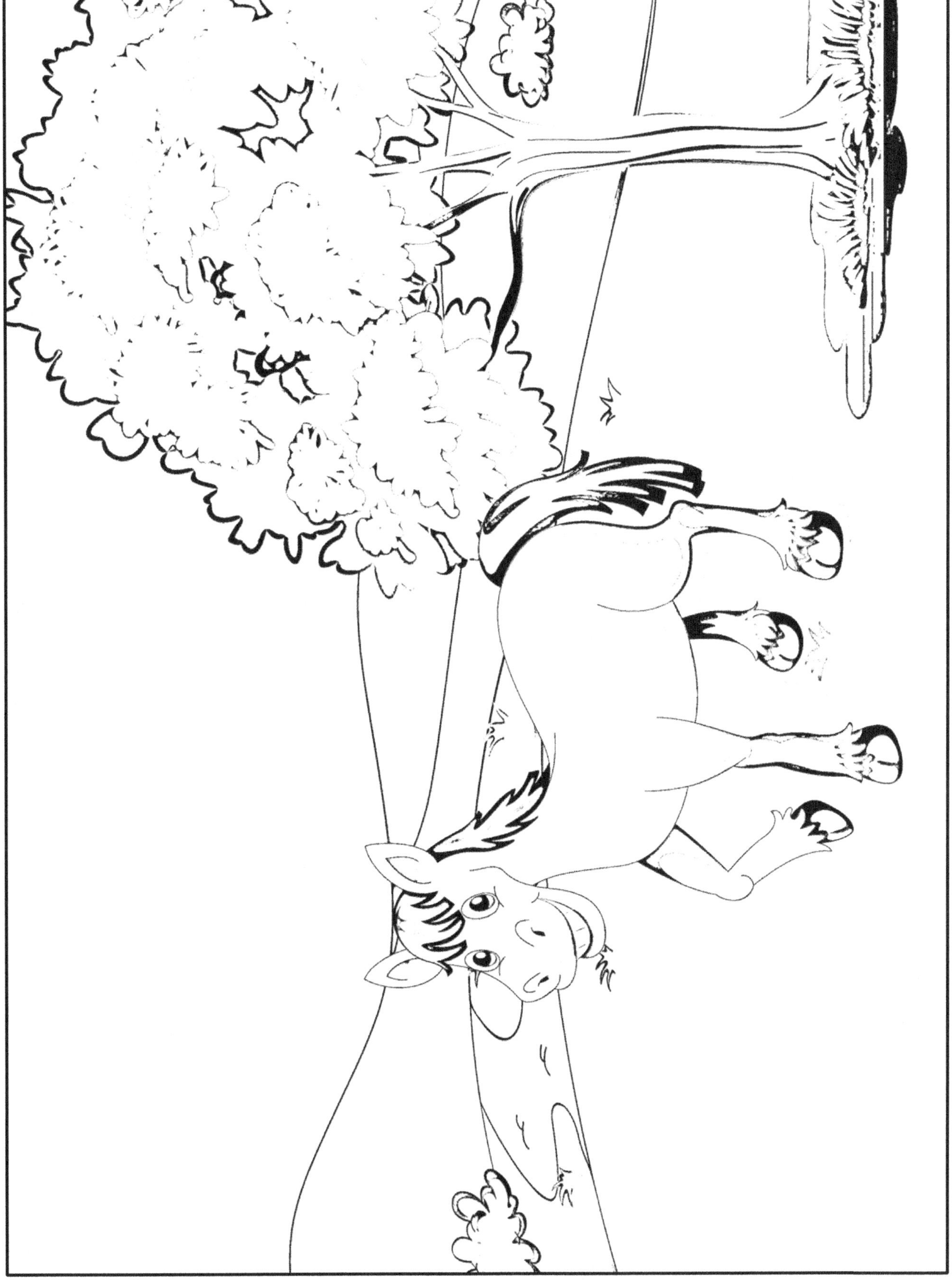

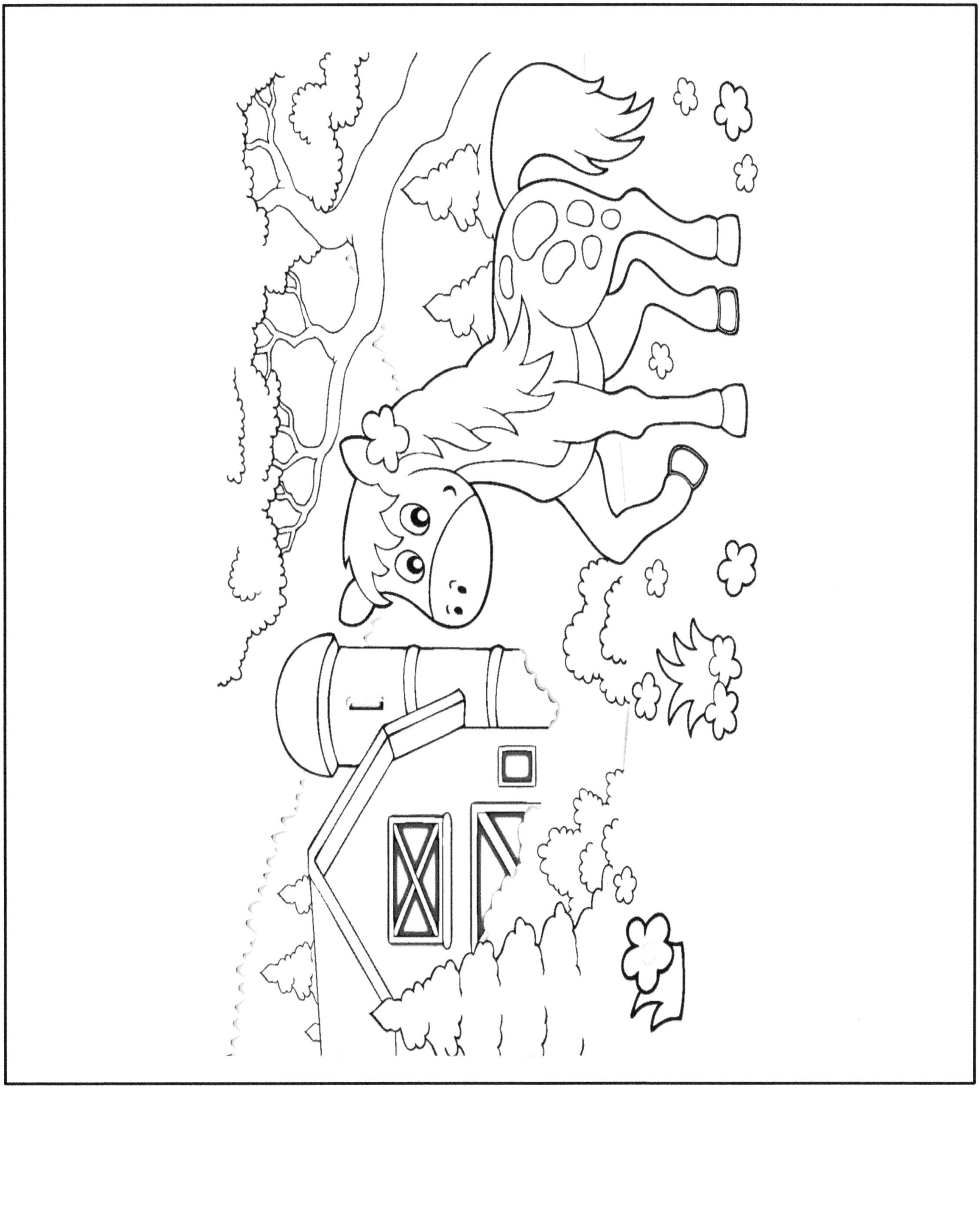

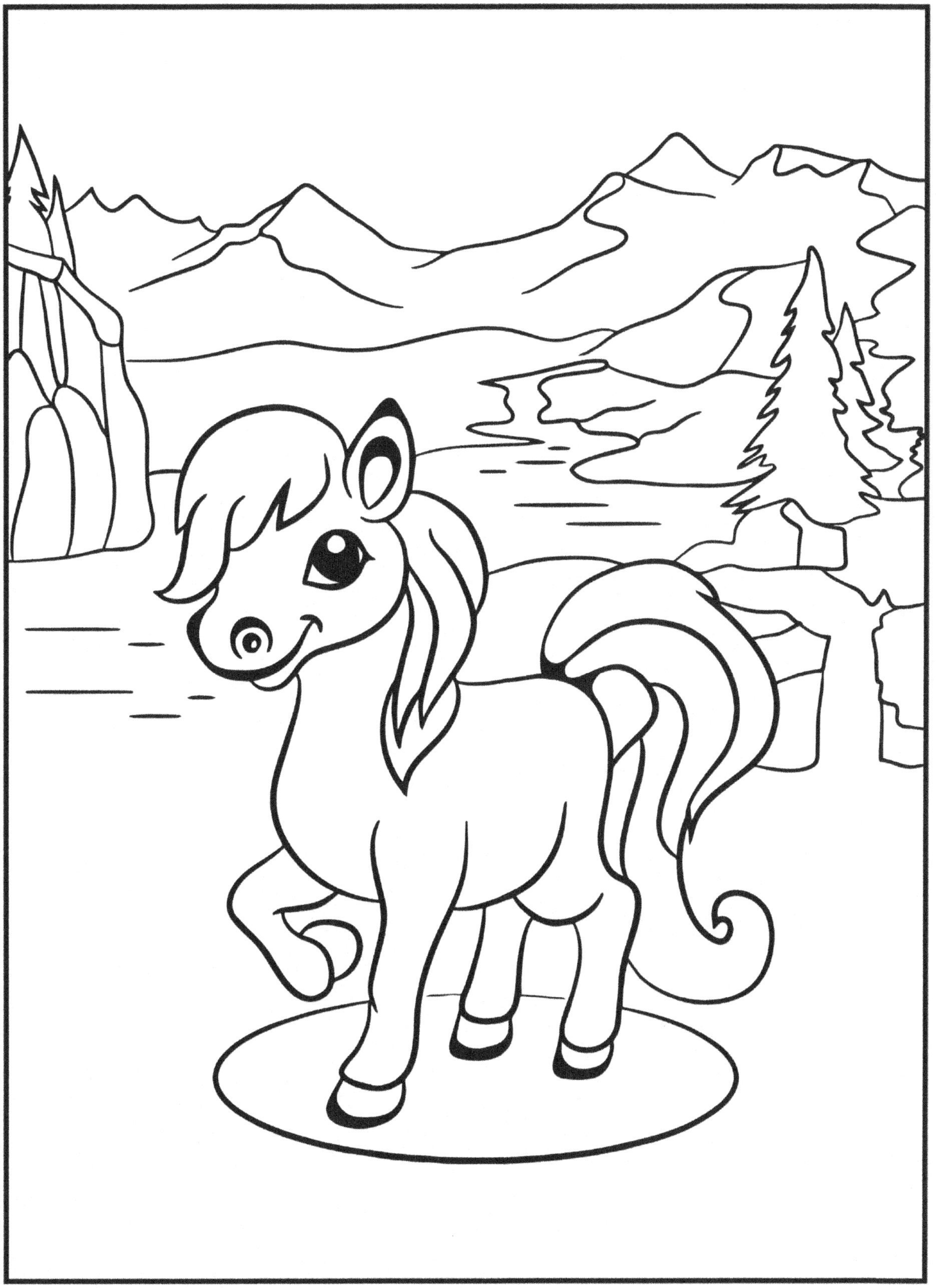

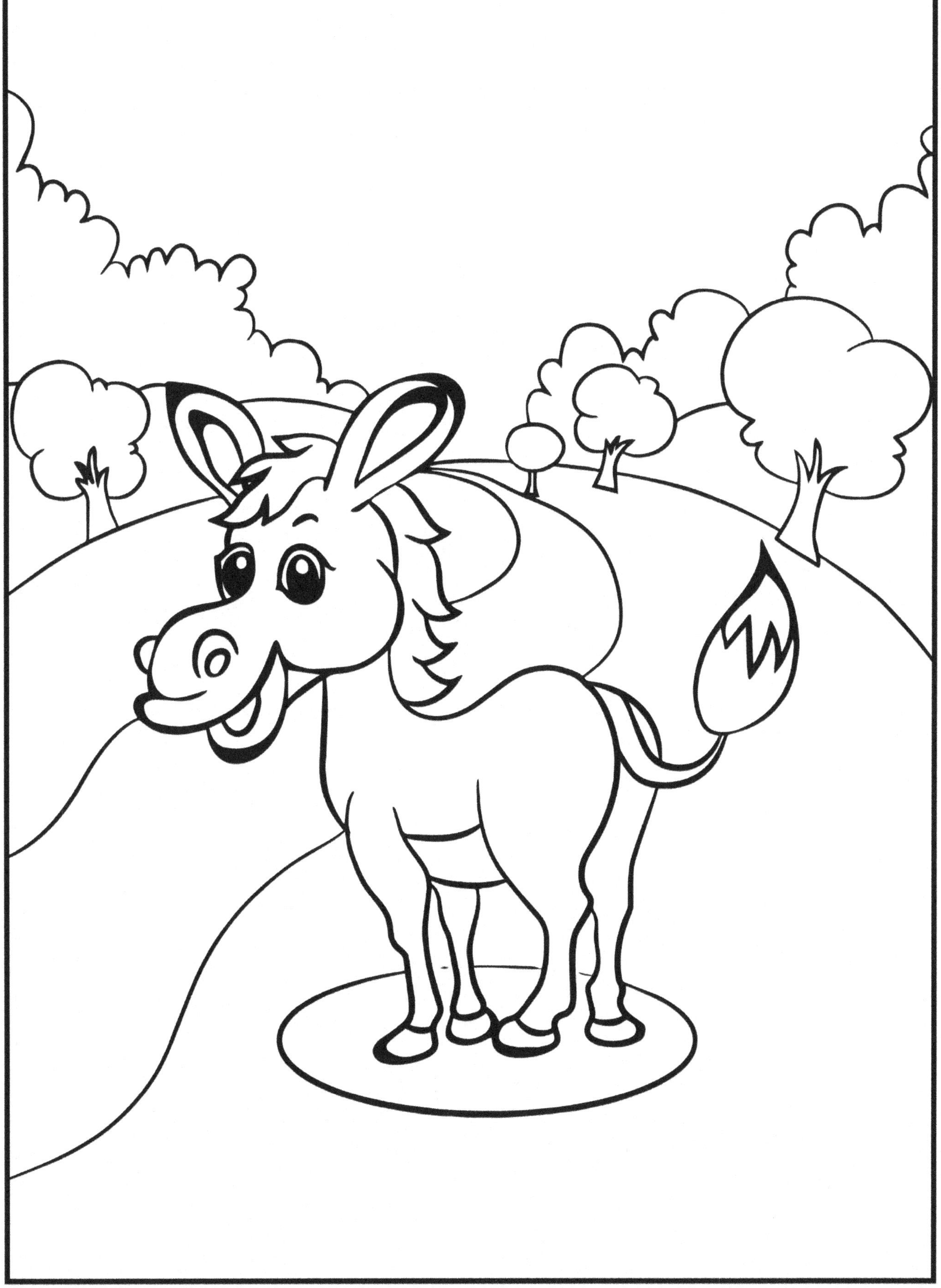

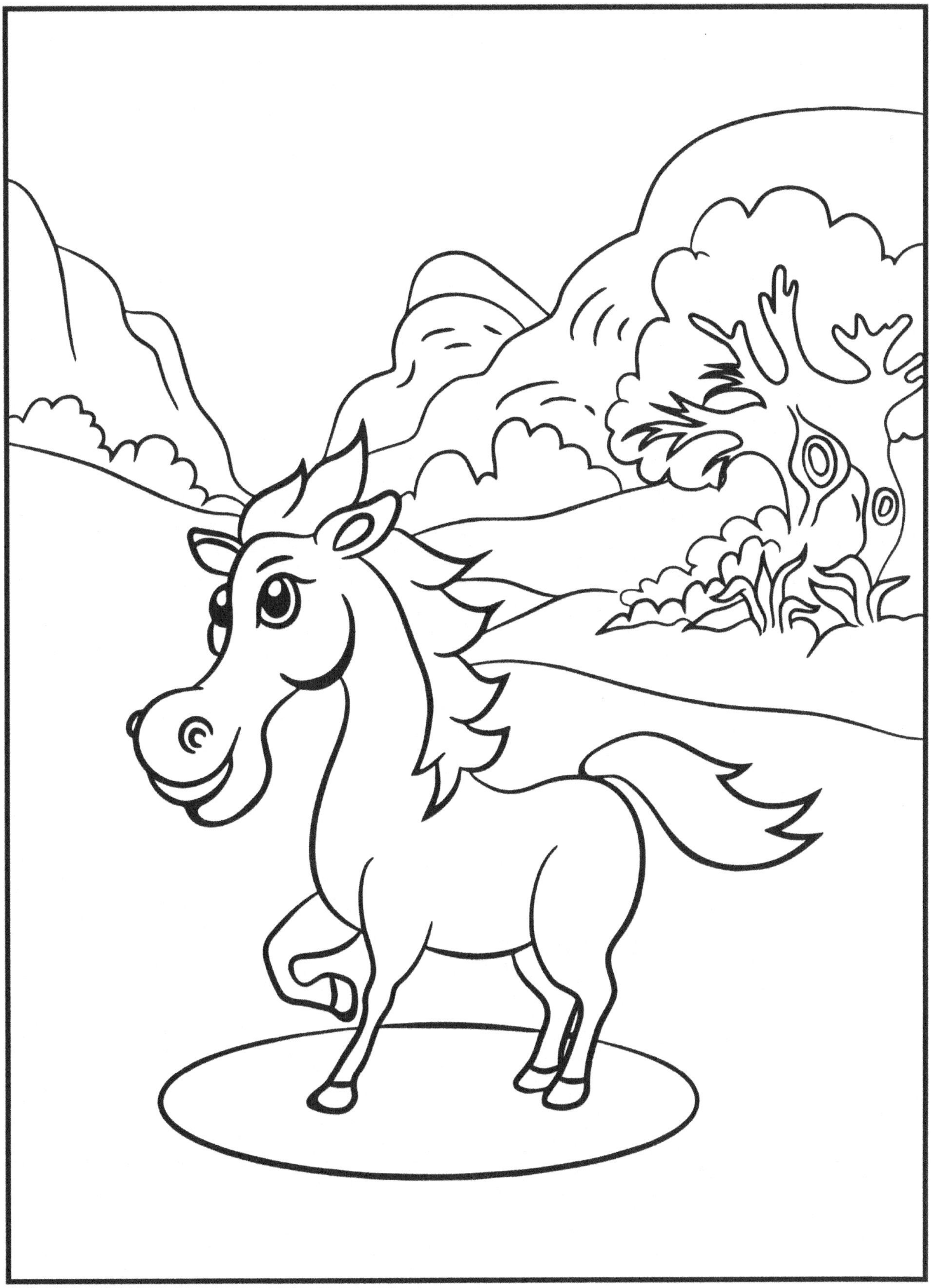

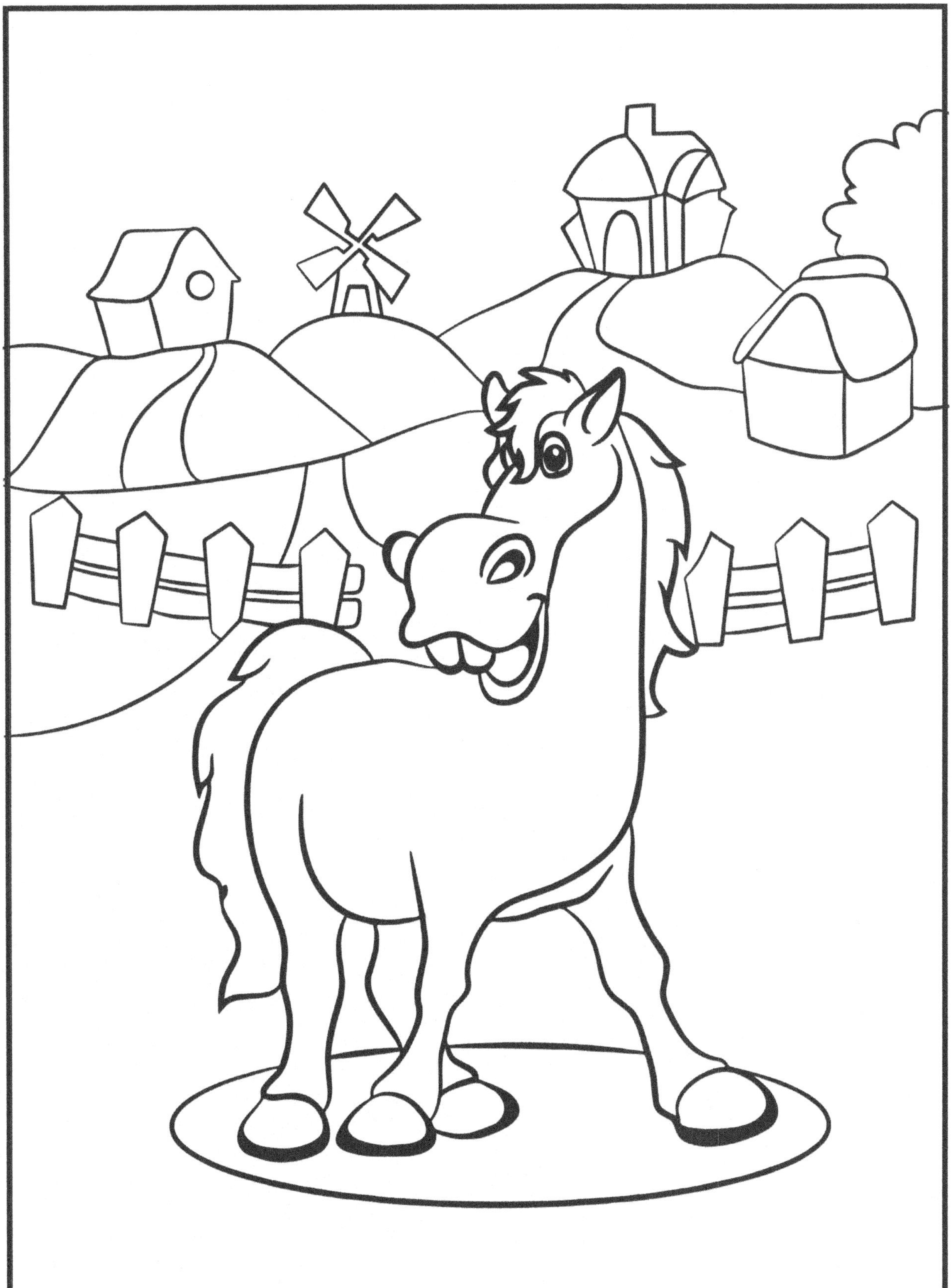

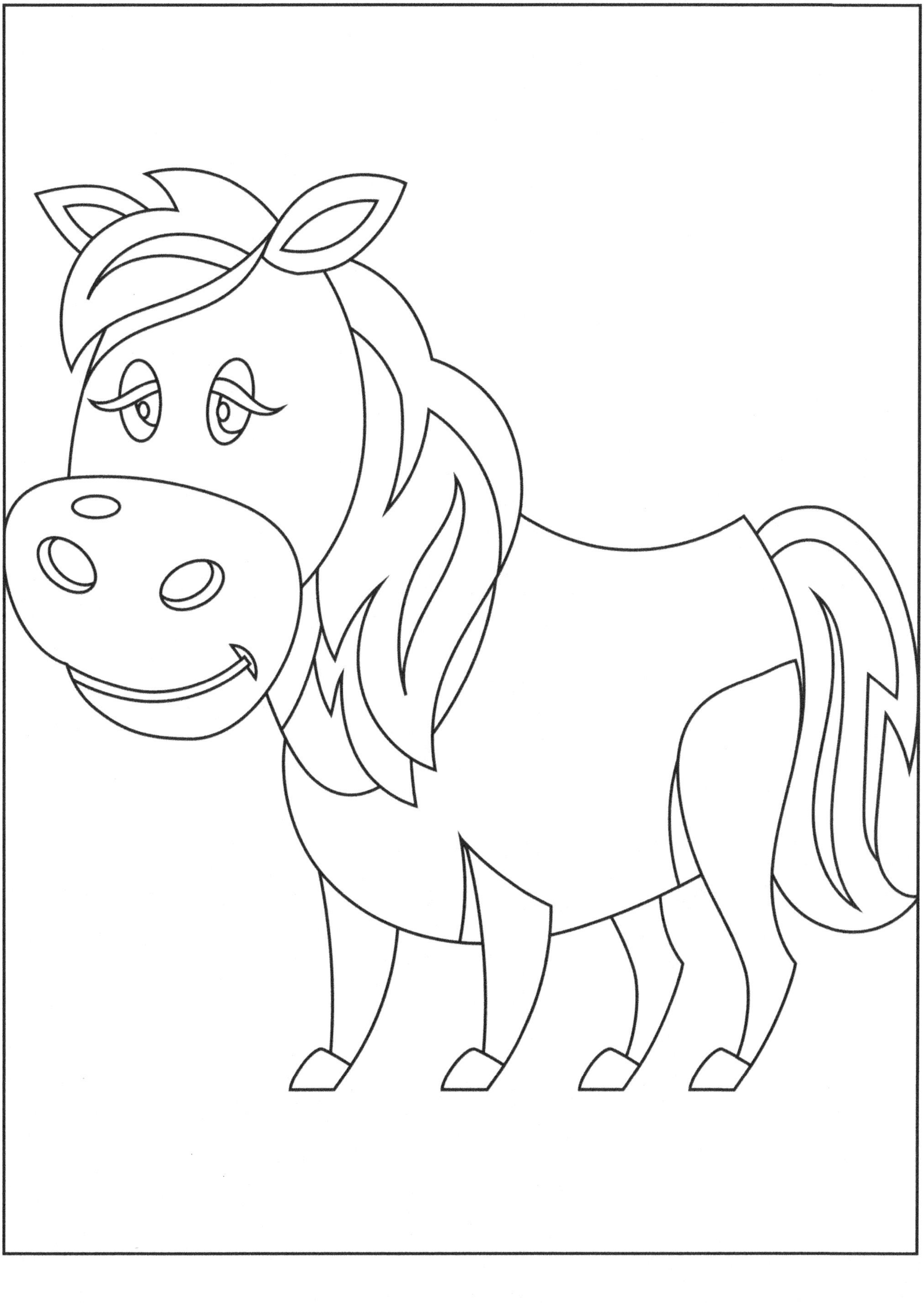

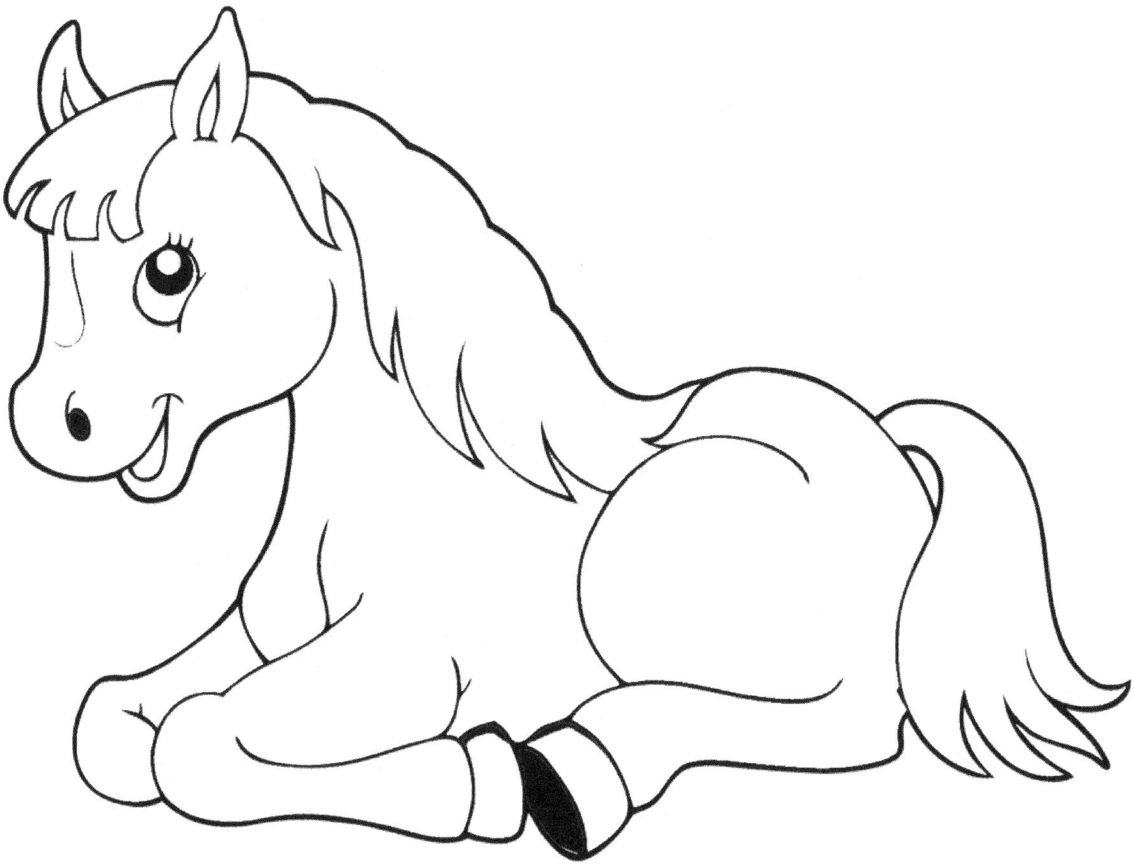

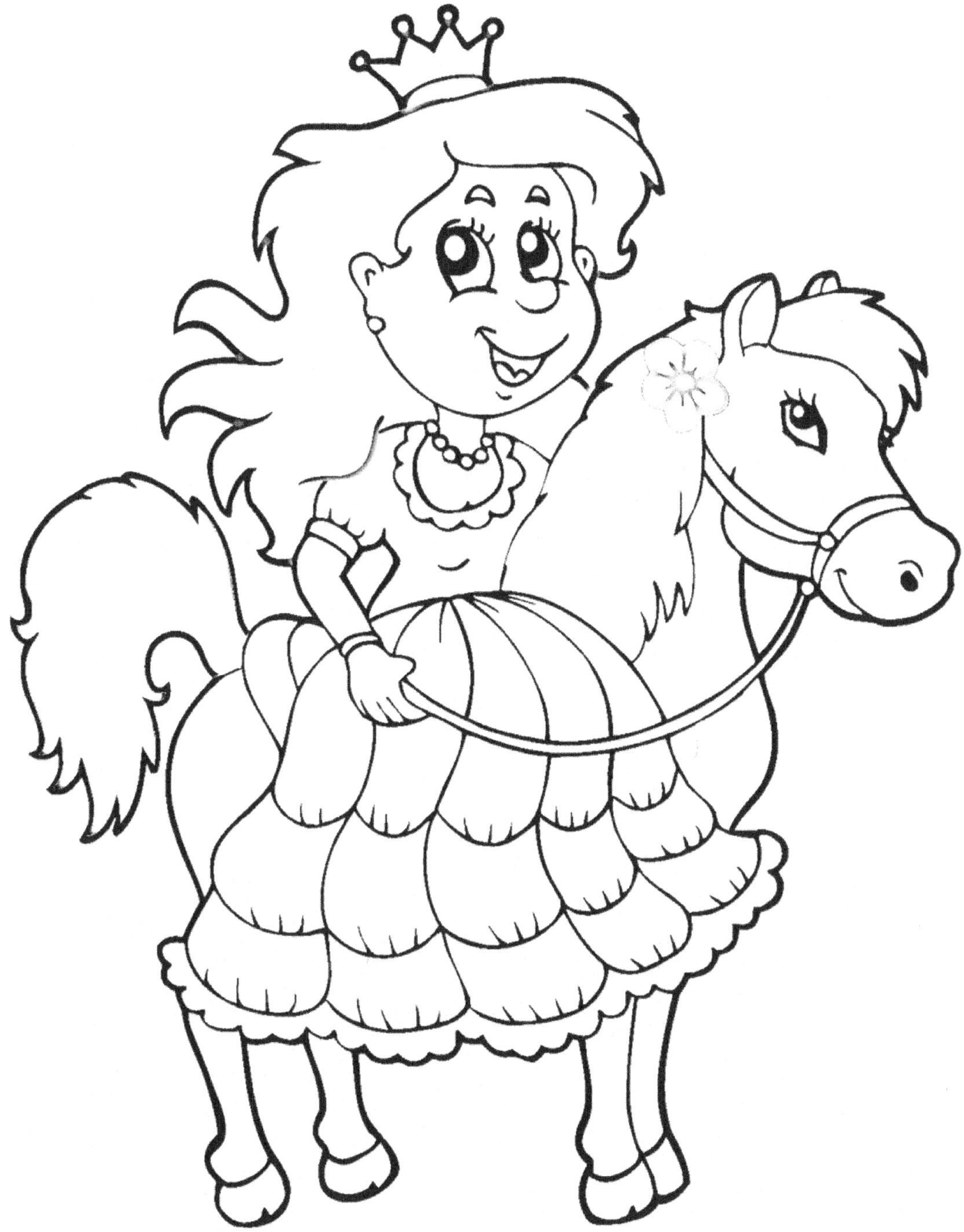

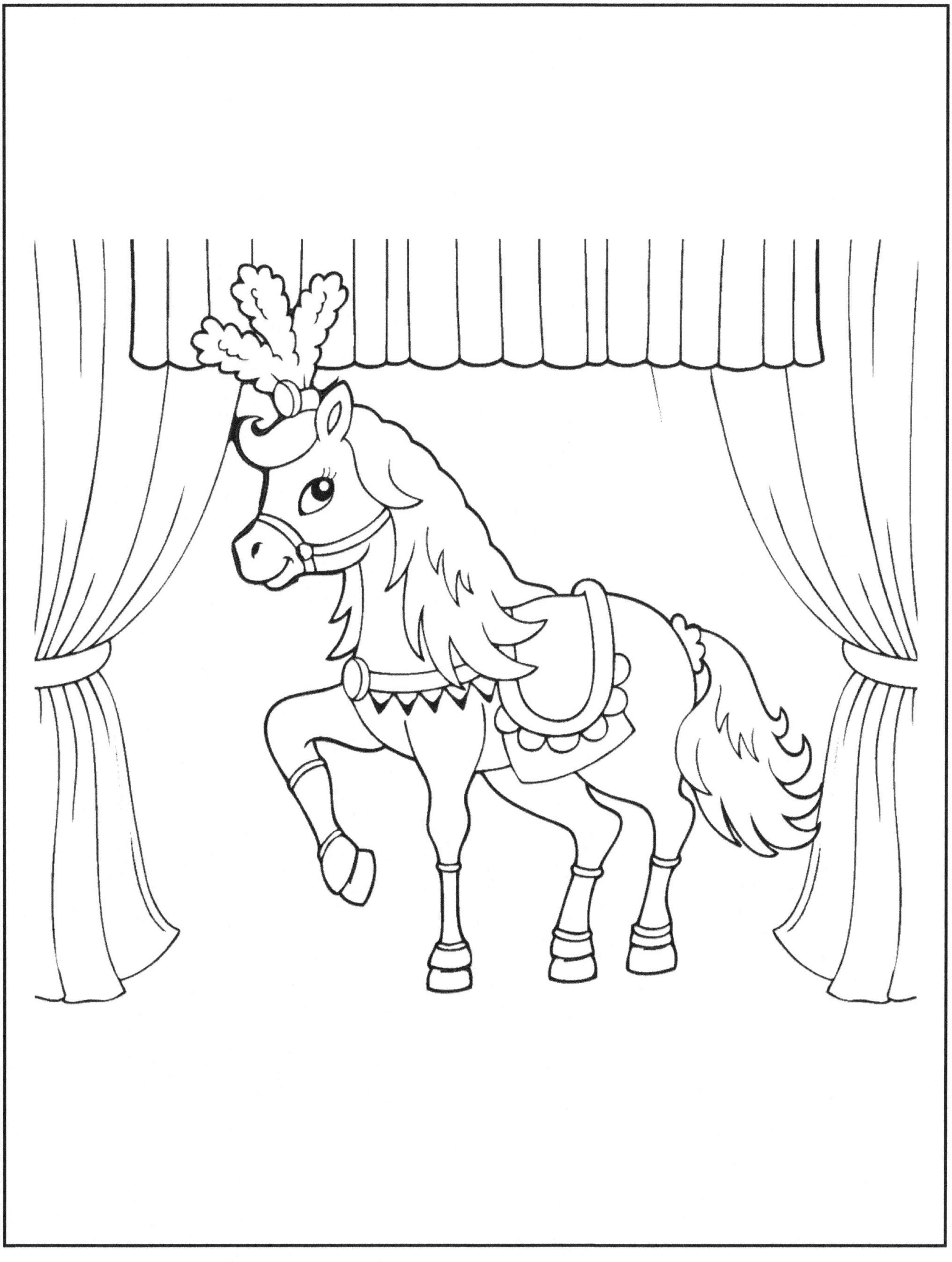

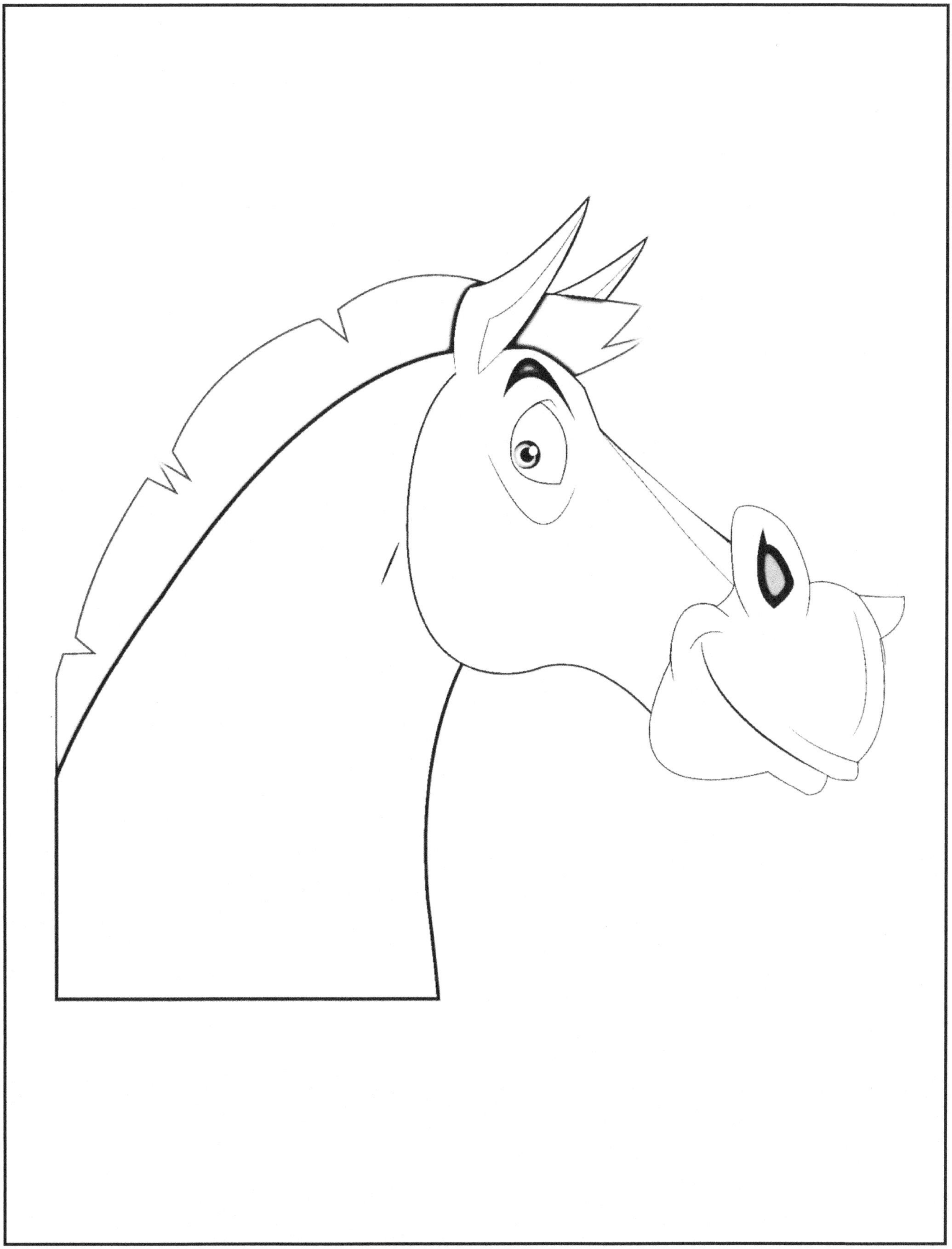

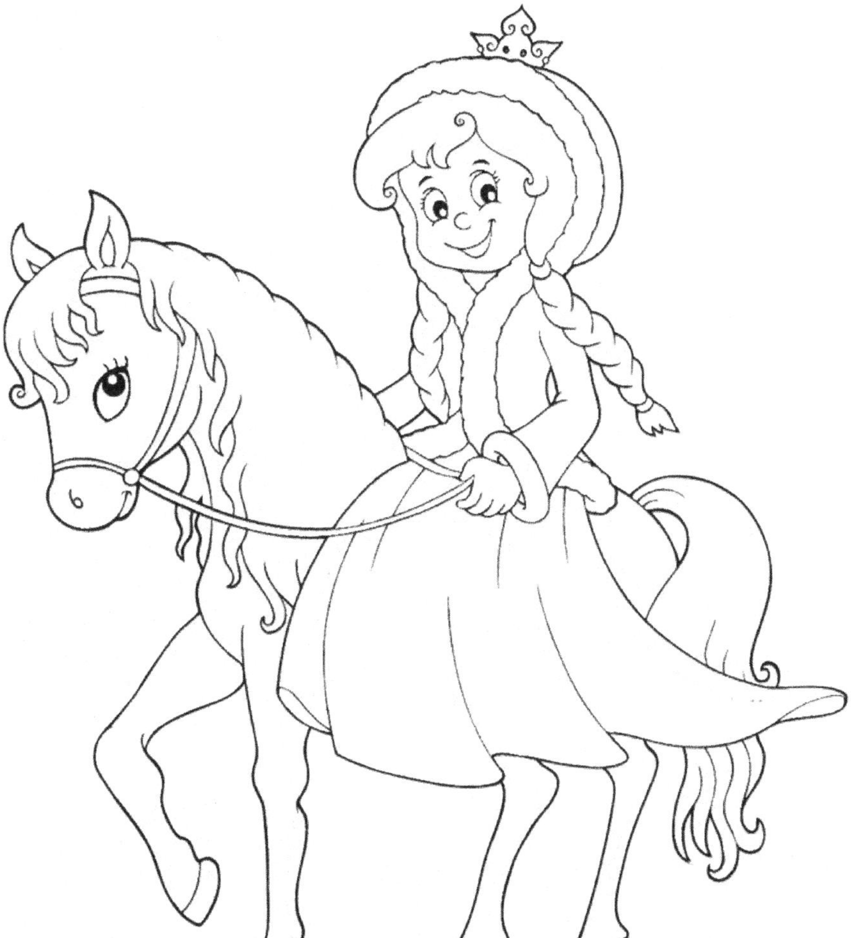

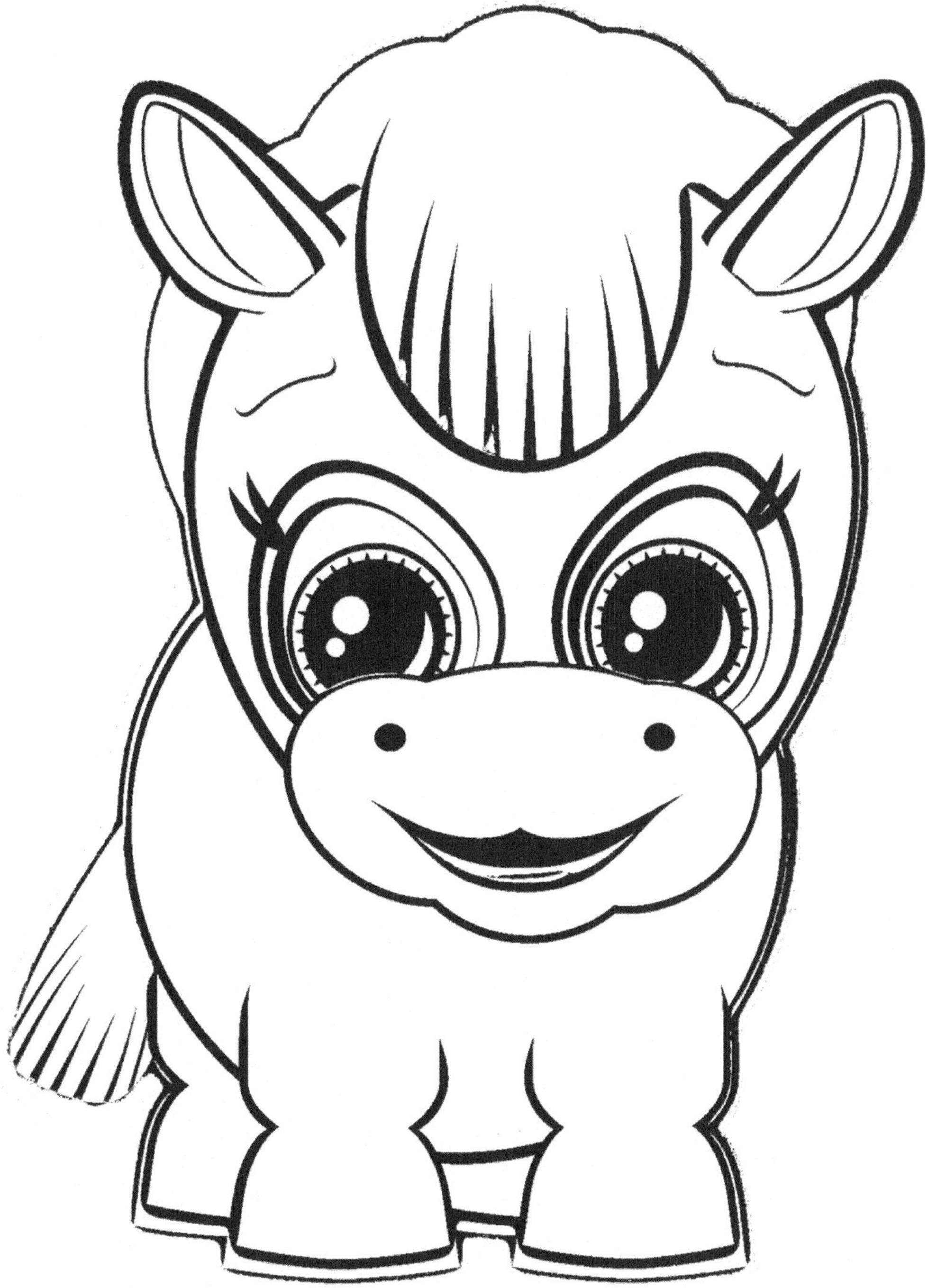

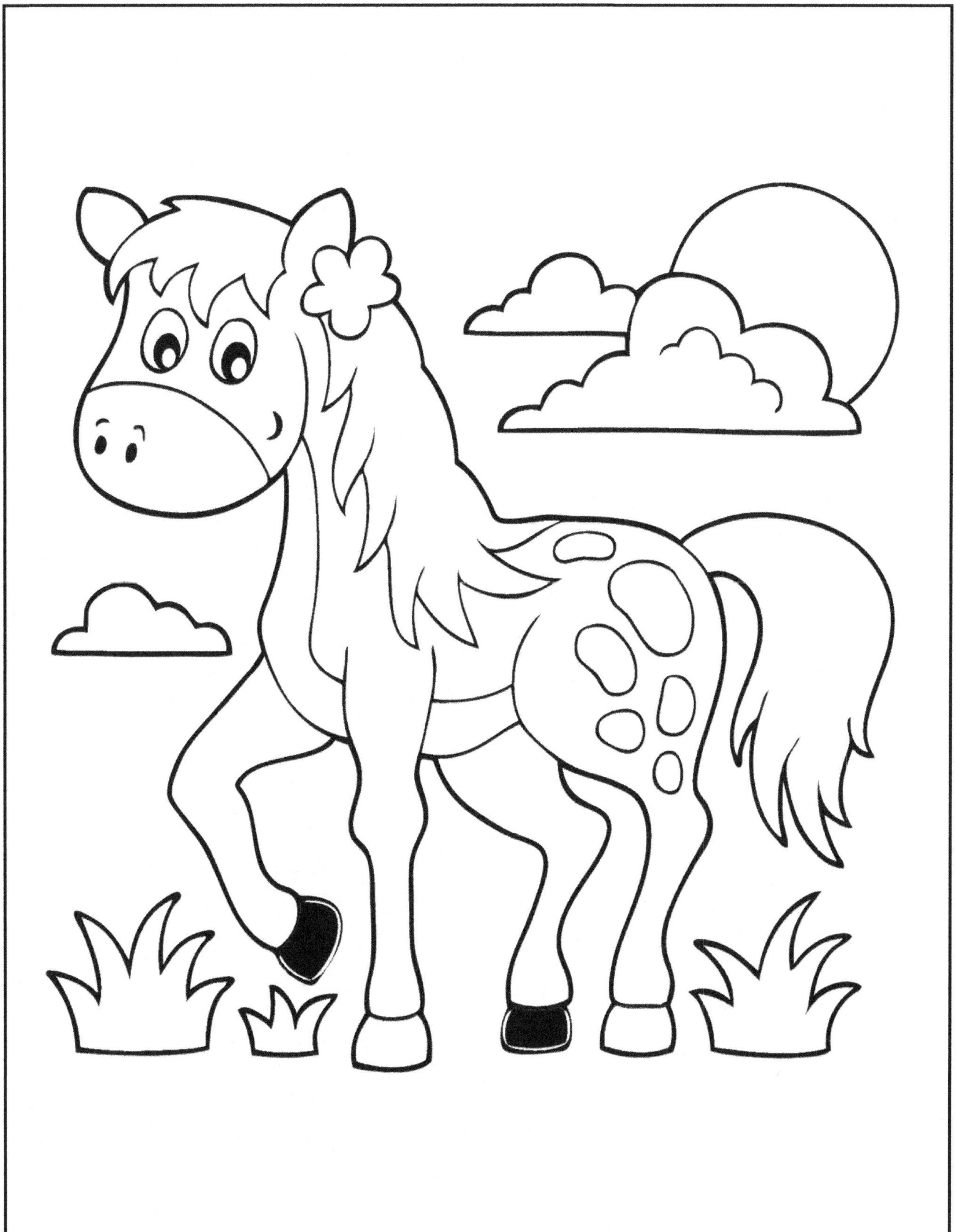

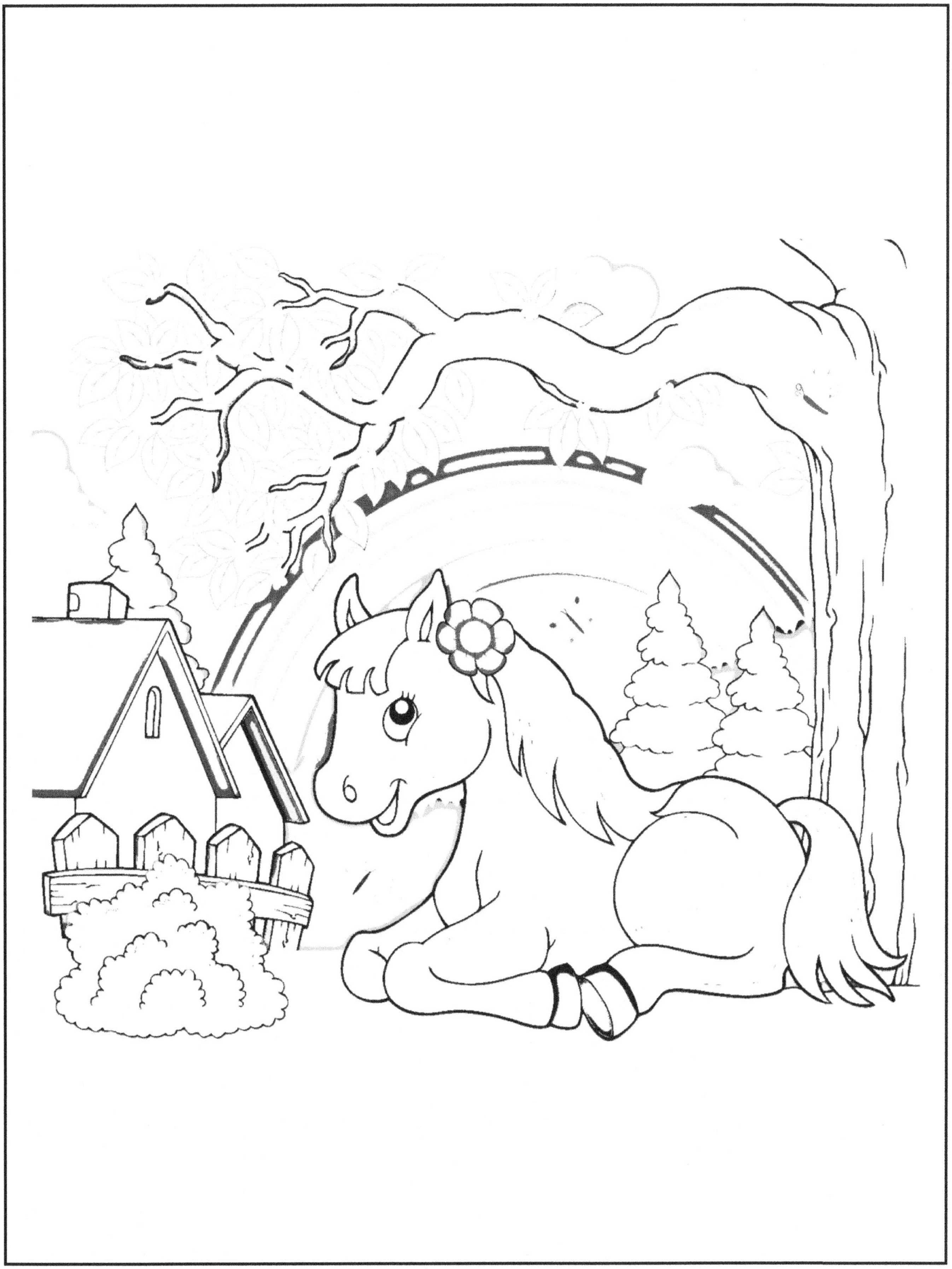

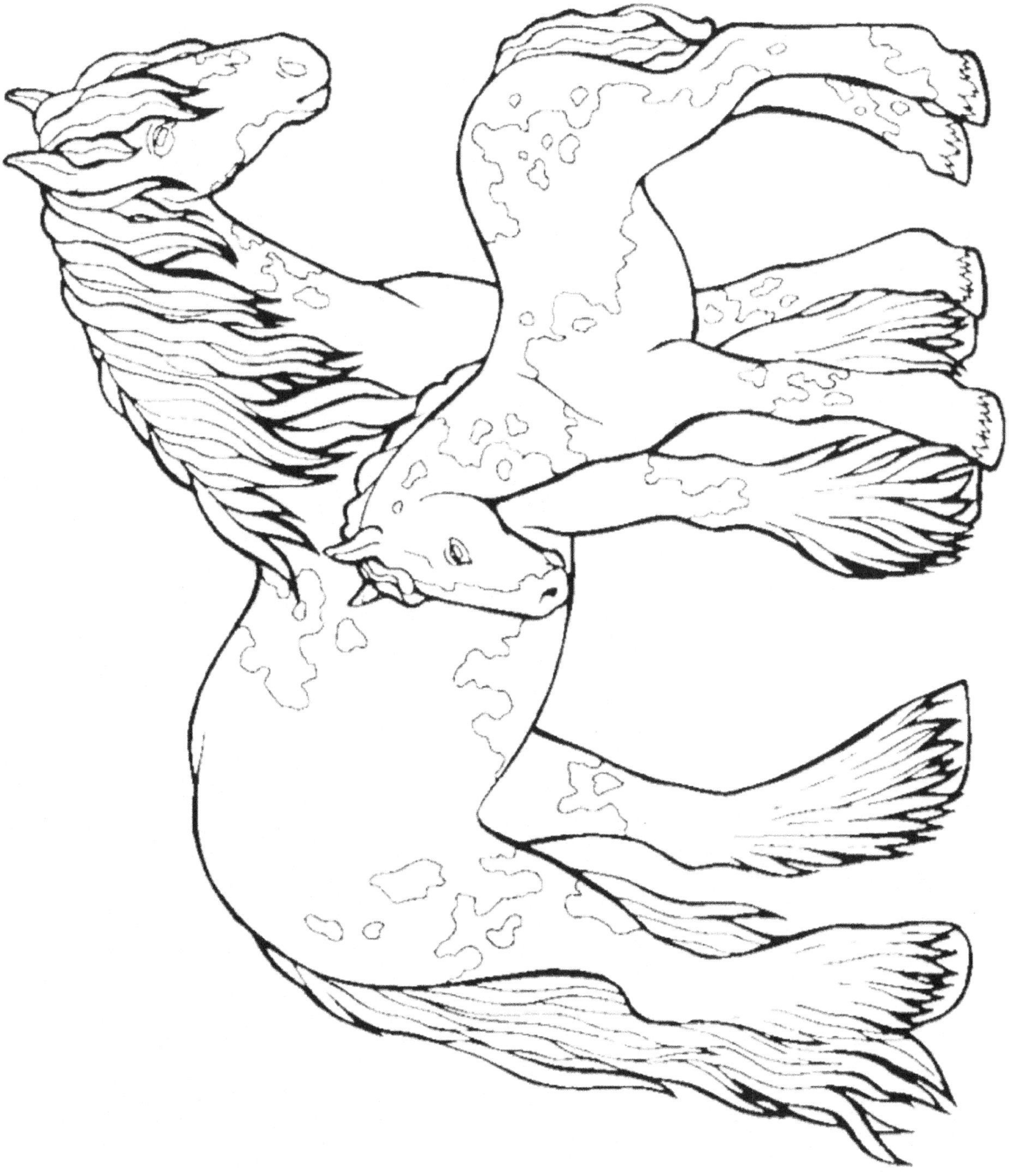

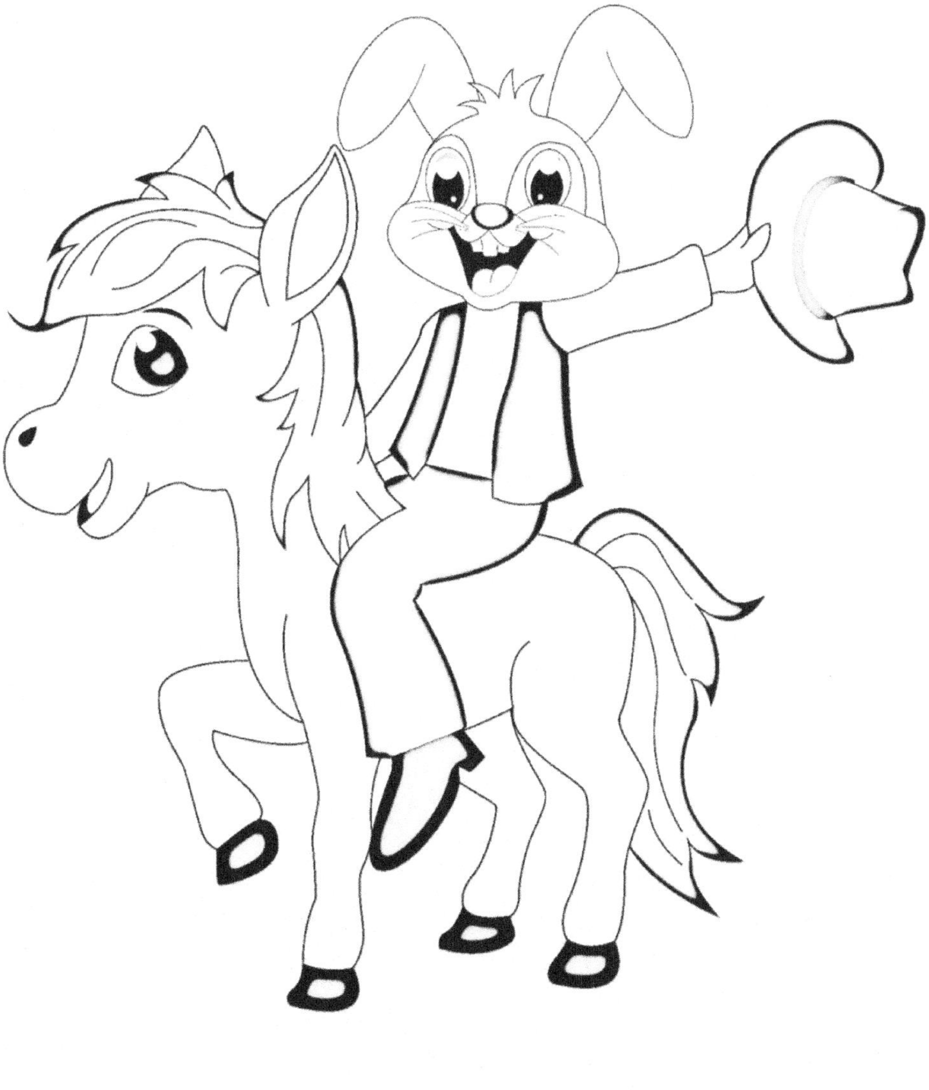

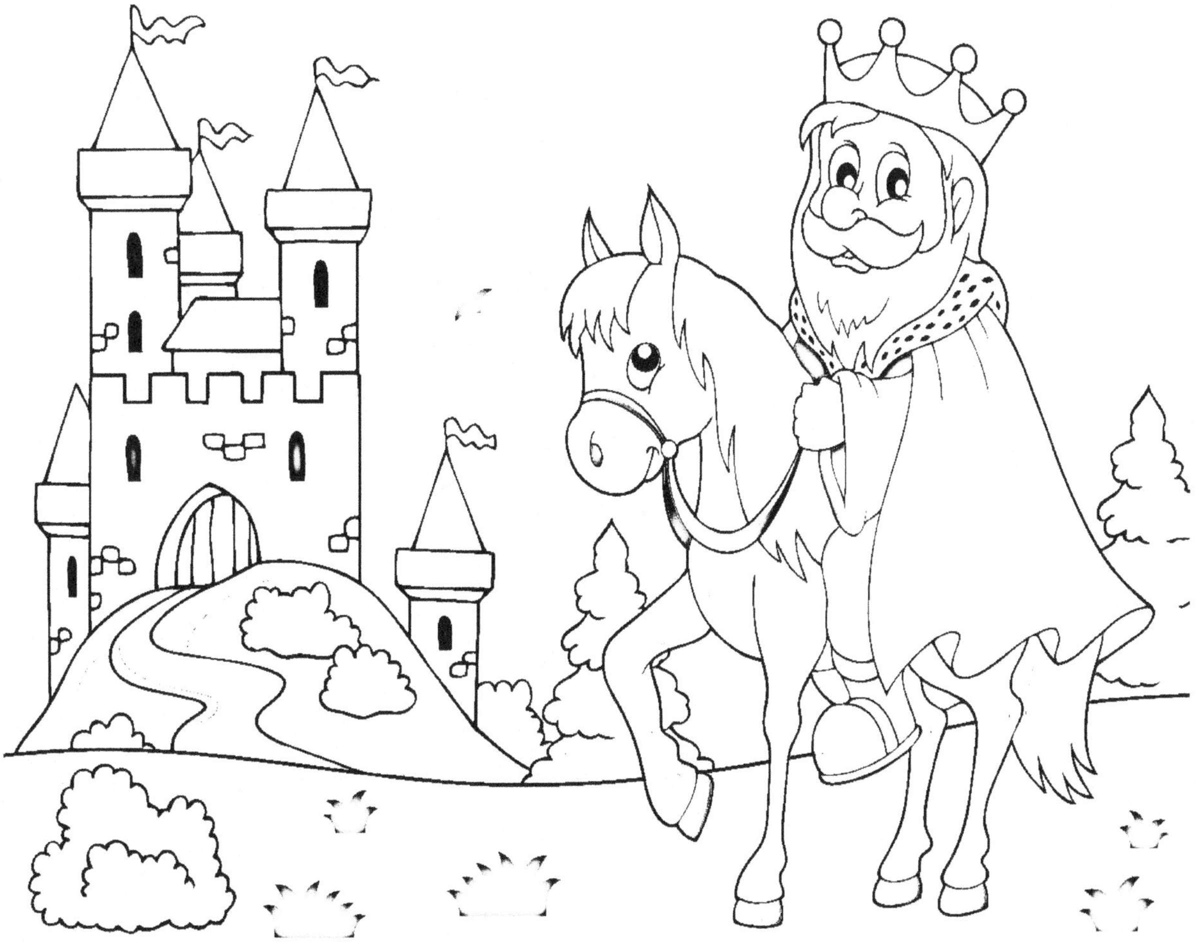

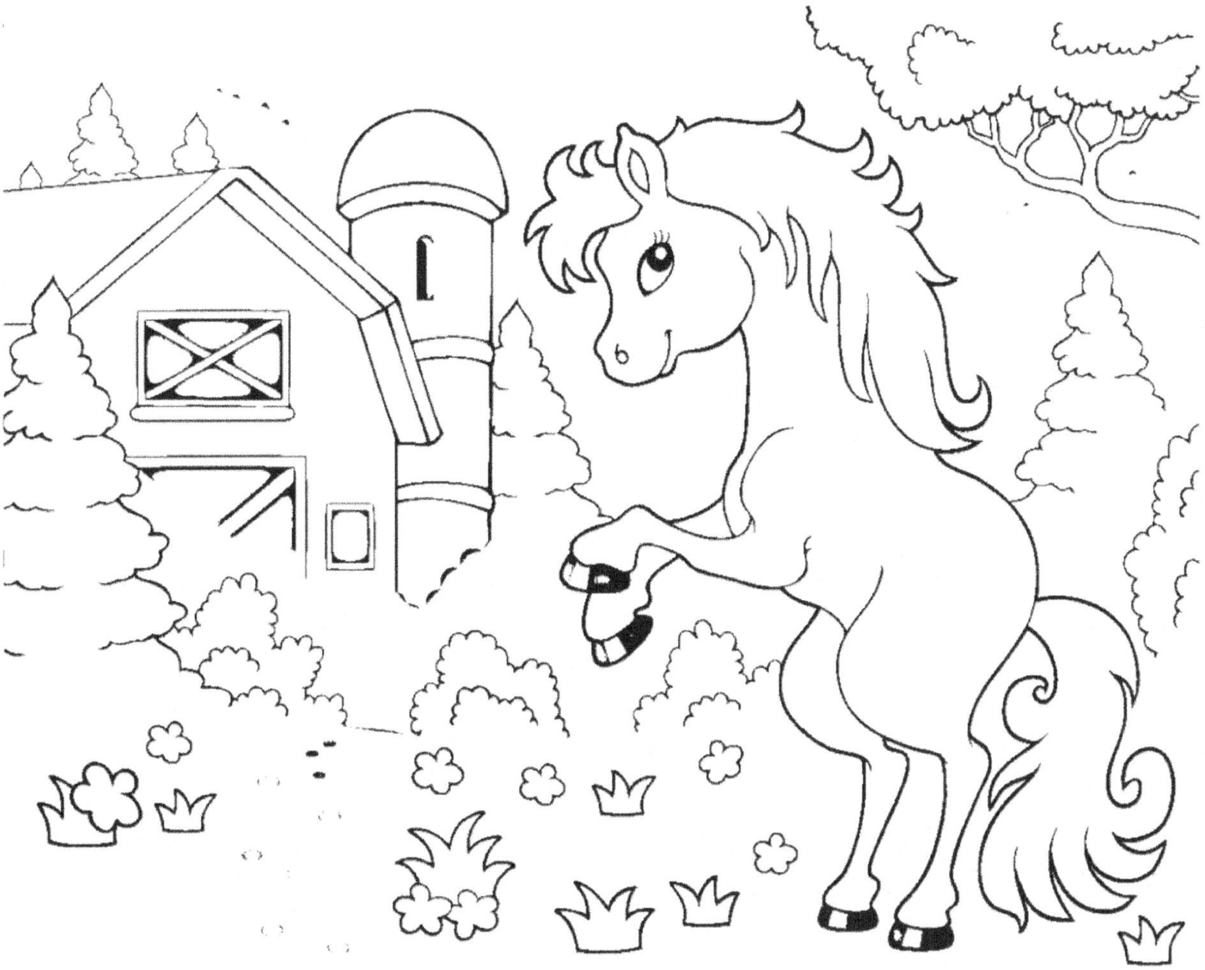

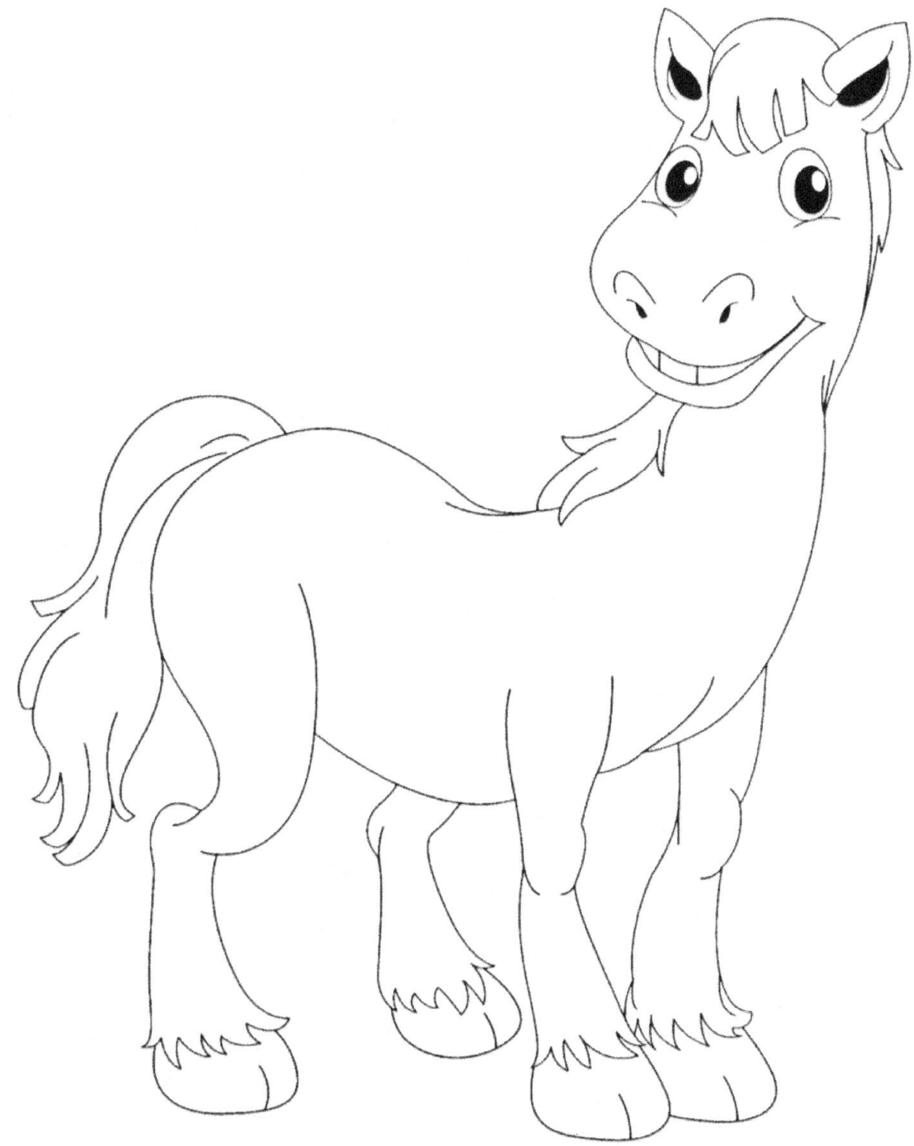

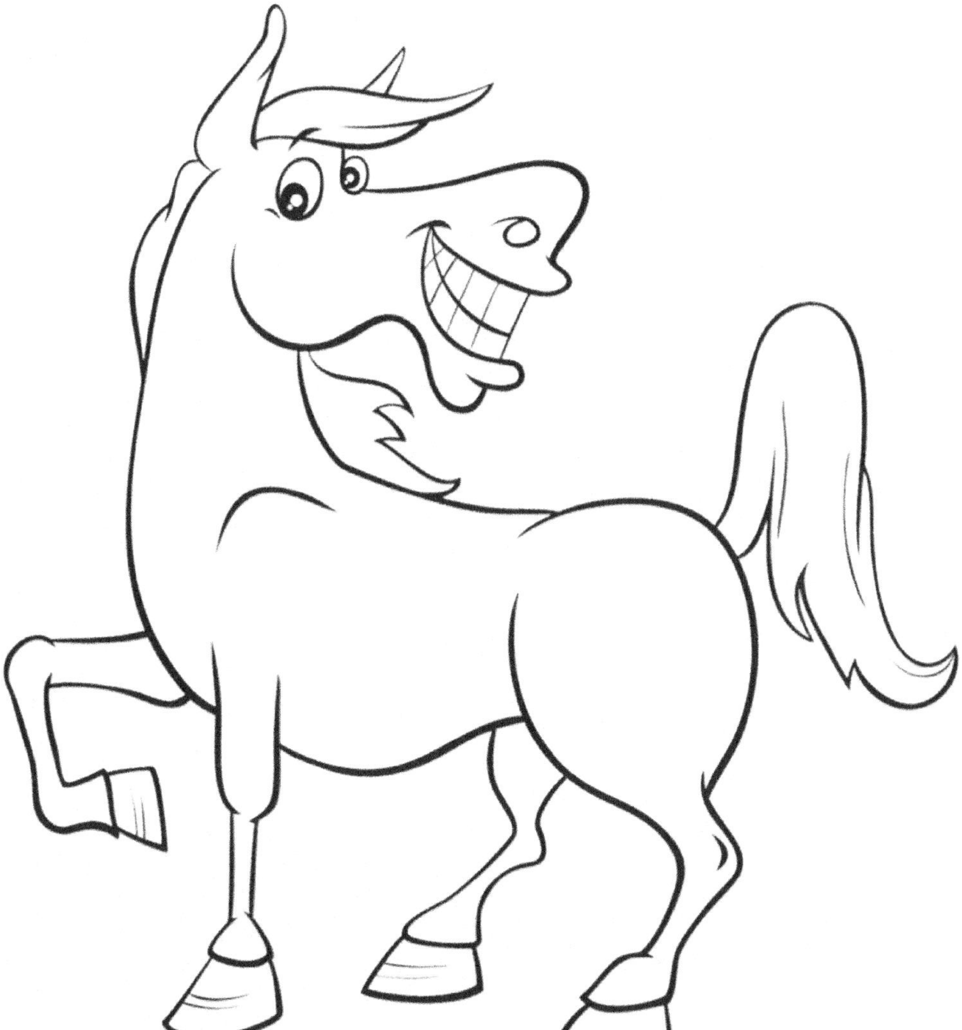

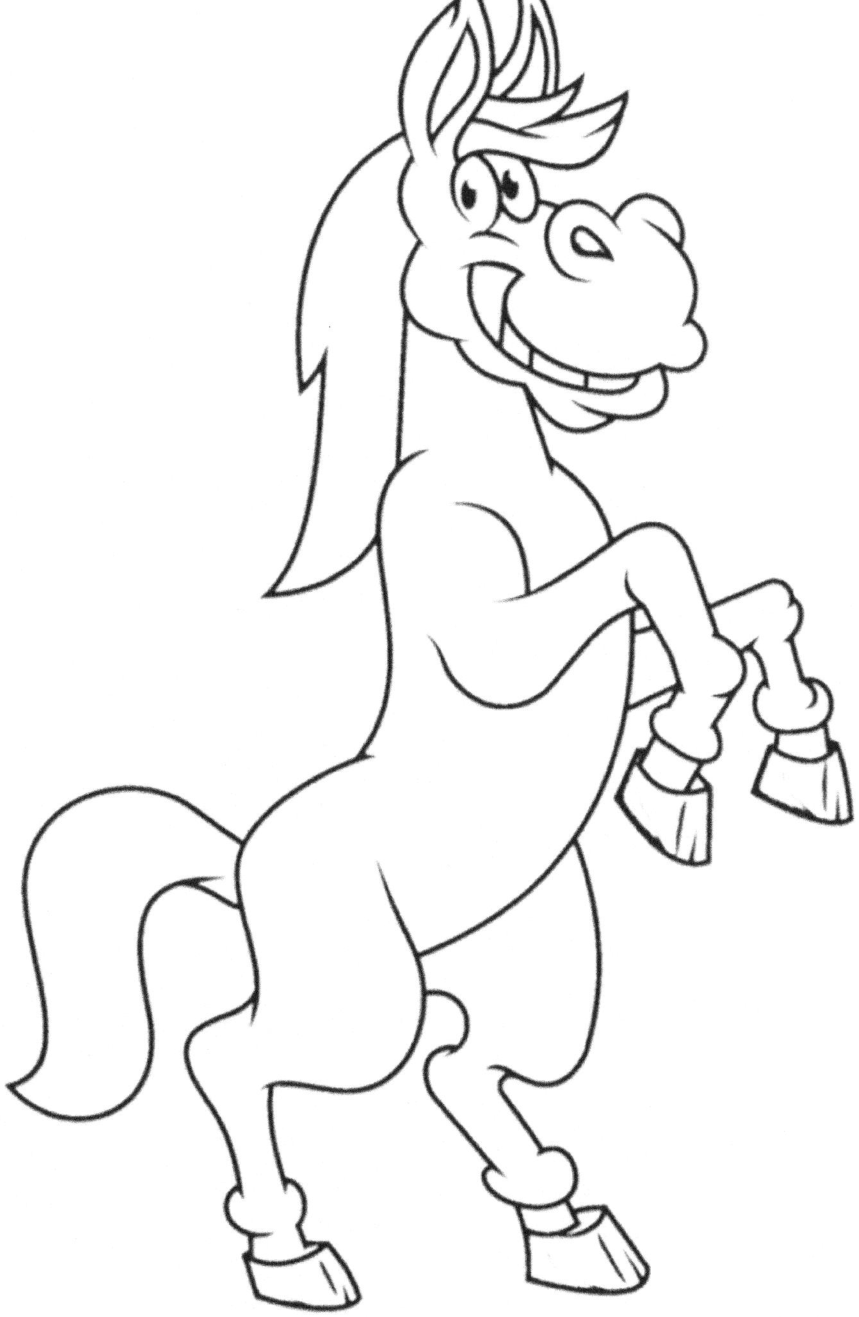

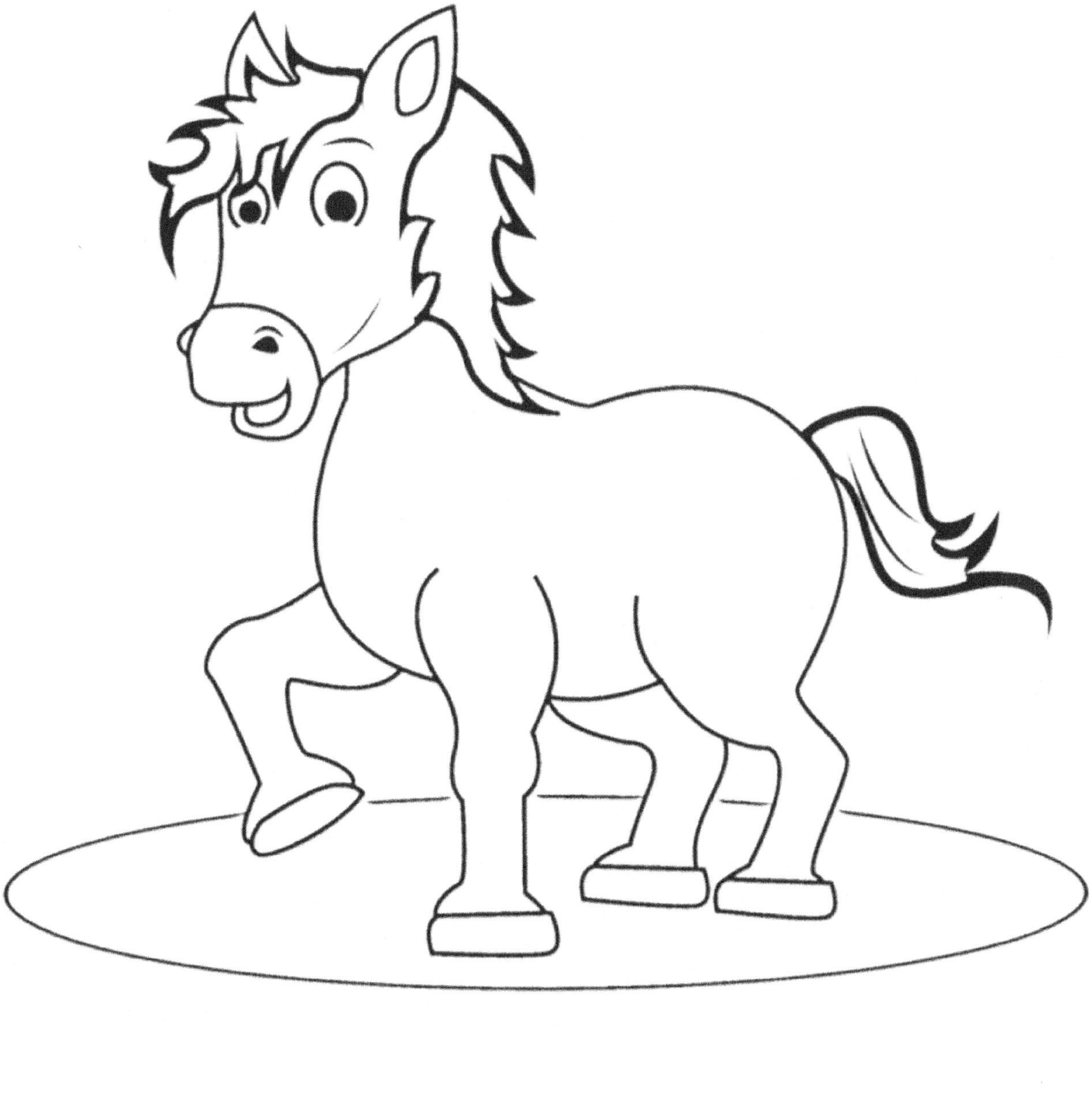

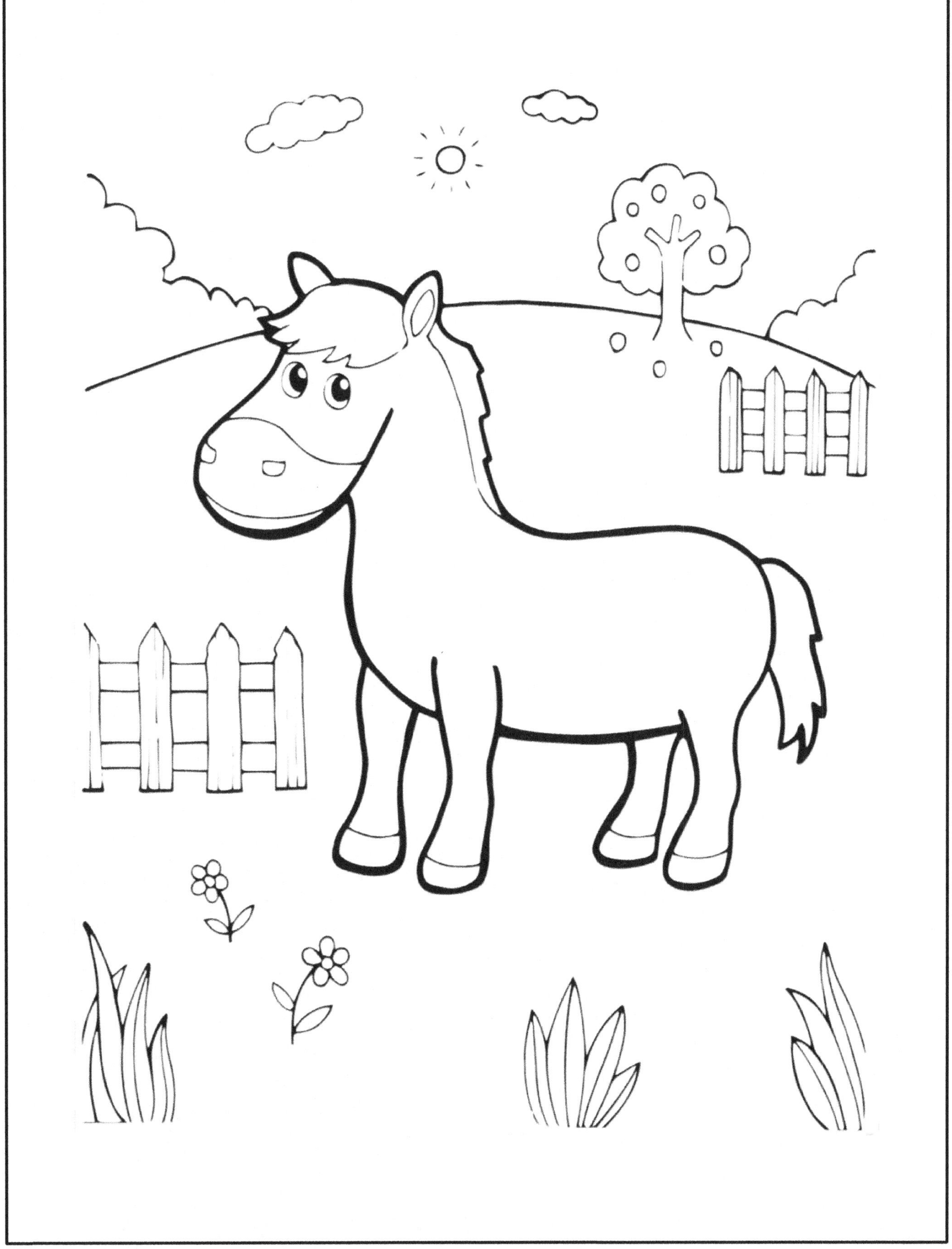

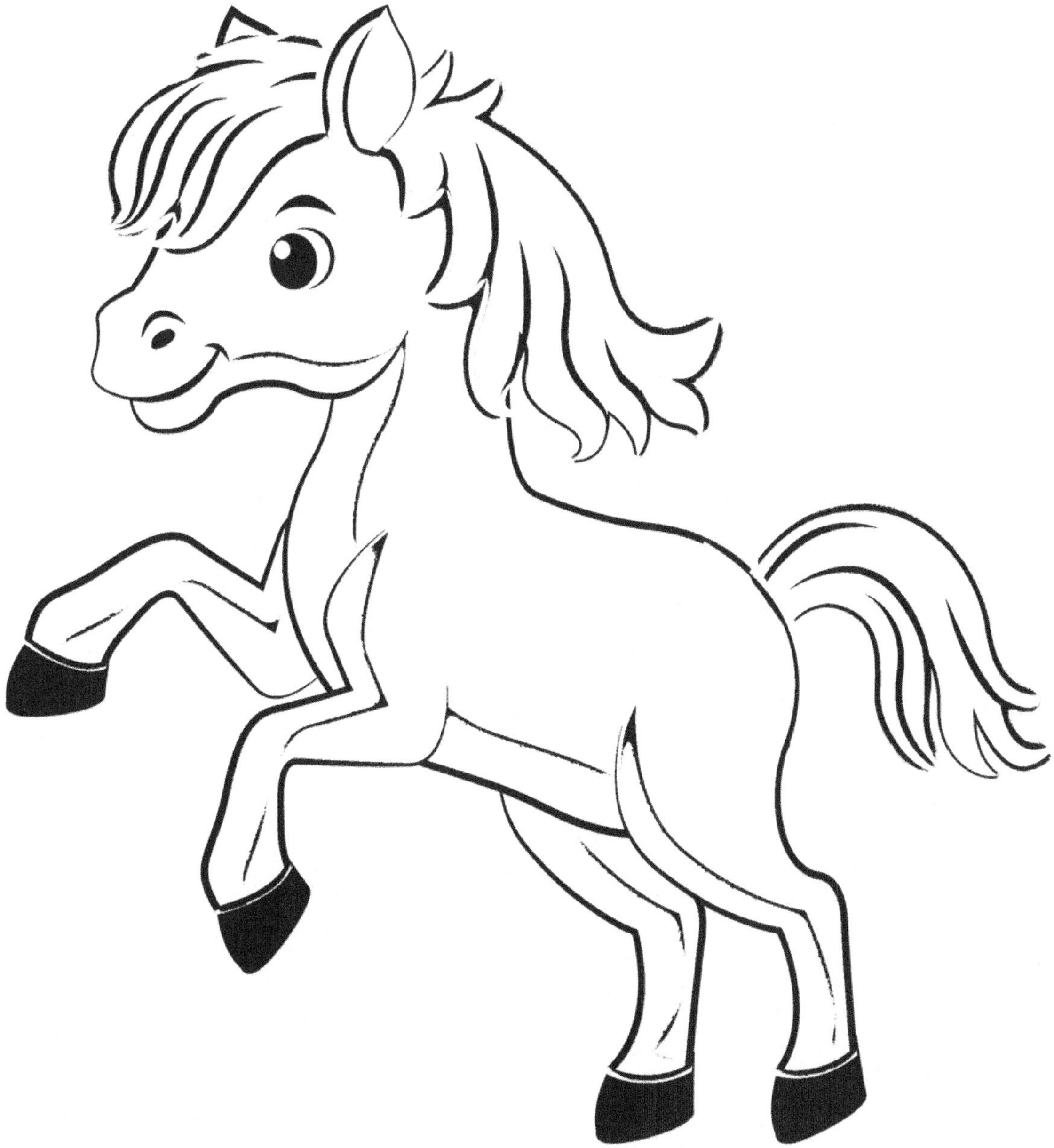

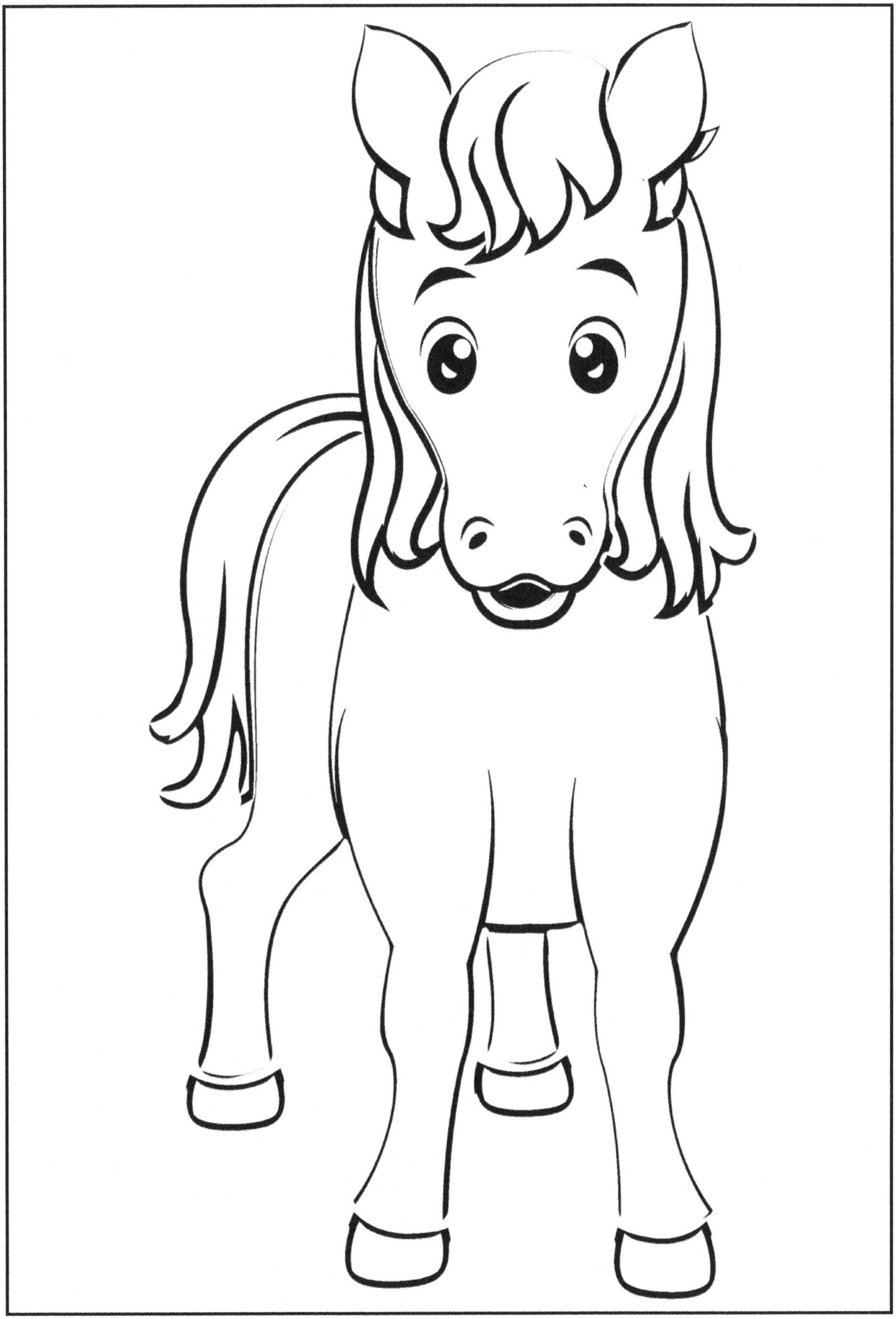

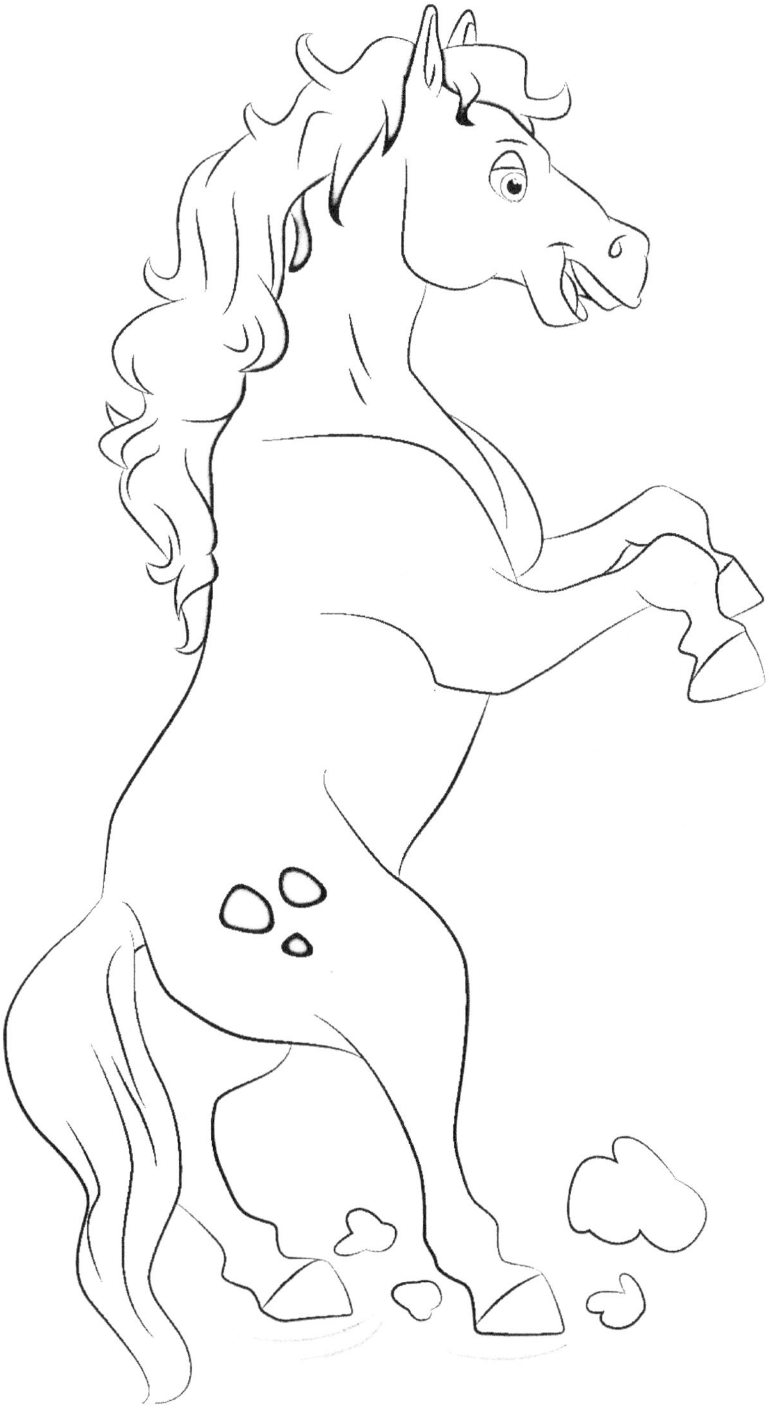

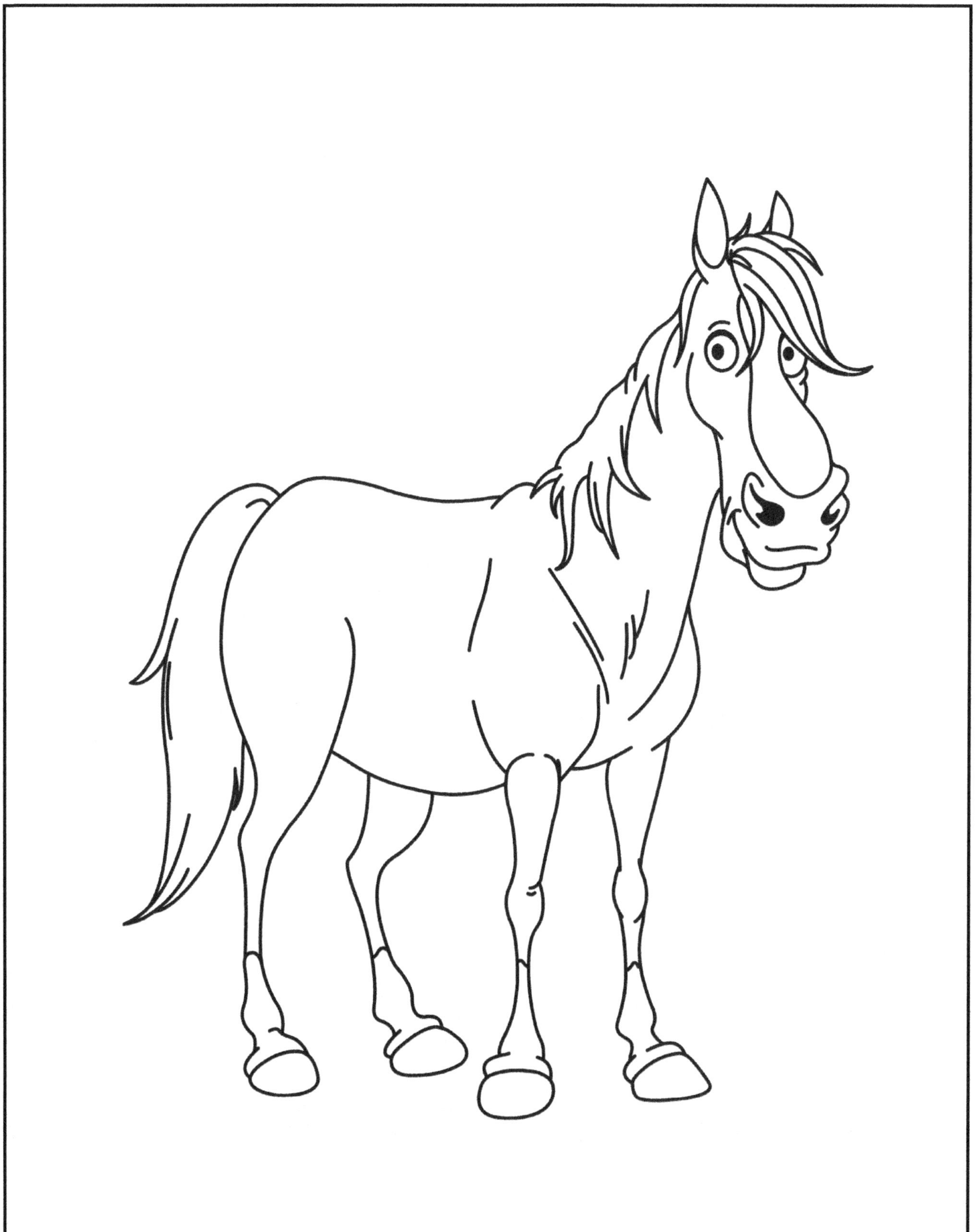

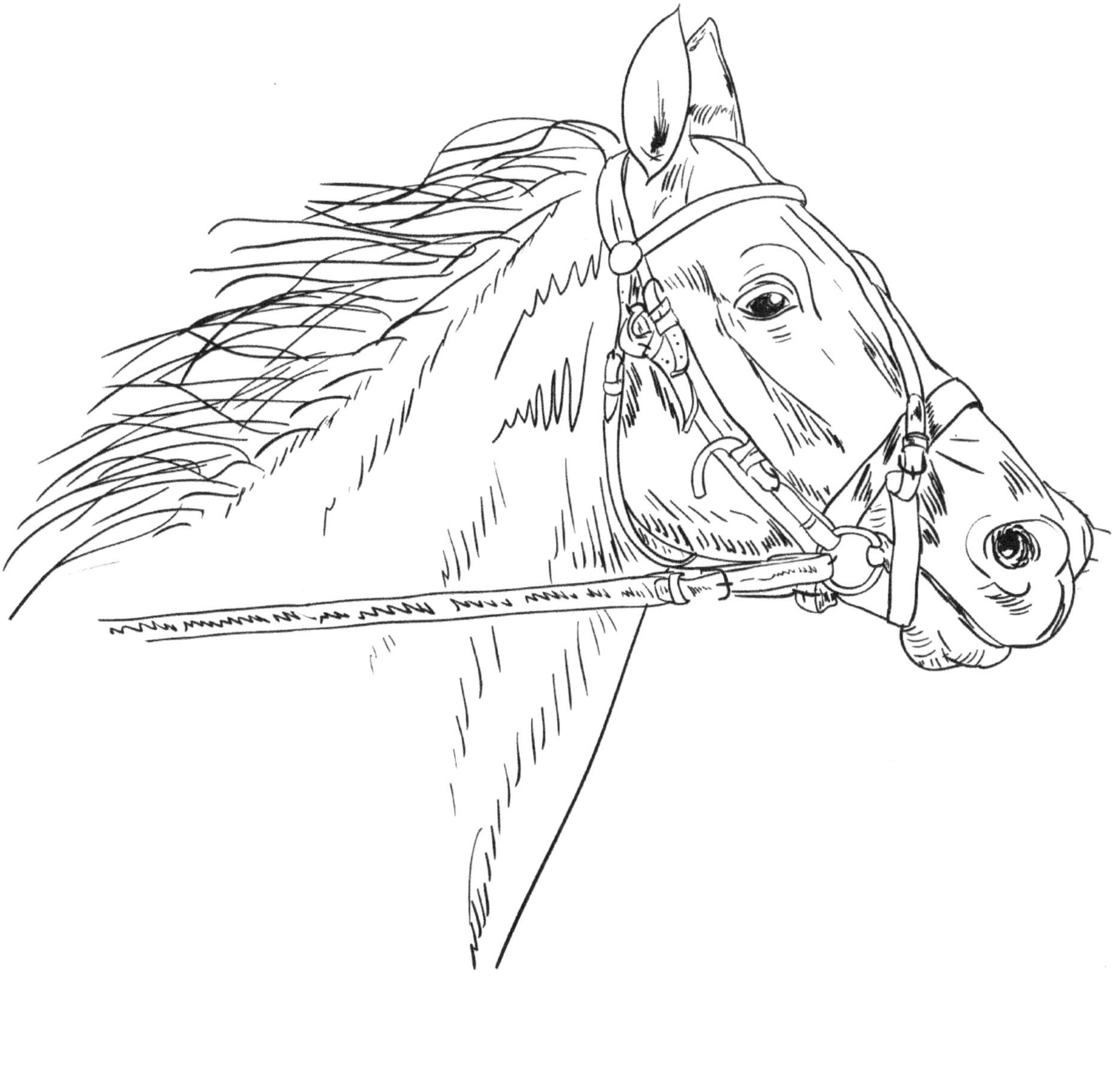

Made in the USA
Coppell, TX
26 March 2021

52122952R00057